SPIRITUAL DIRECTION
AND
MIDLIFE DEVELOPMENT

SPIRITUAL DIRECTION
AND
MIDLIFE DEVELOPMENT

Raymond Studzinski, O.S.B.

A Campion Book

Loyola University Press
Chicago

©1985 St. Meinrad Archabbey
ISBN 0-8294-0481-3
Printed in the United States of America
Designed by C. L. Tornatore

Library of Congress Cataloging in Publication Data

Studzinski, Raymond, 1943–
  Spiritual direction and midlife development.

  Bibliography: p. 139
  Includes index.
  1. Middle age—Religious life.   2. Spiritual direction.   3. Middle age—
Psychological aspects.   I. Title.
BV4579.5.S78   1985   248   85-10
ISBN 0-8294-0481-3

To my parents

Contents

Preface ix

1 The Spiritual Challenge of Midlife 1

2 Psychic Integration and Midlife 28

3 Conversion and Discernment in Midlife 56

4 Images and Stories at Midlife 83

5 Guidelines for Direction of Midlife Adults 122

Bibliography 139

Index 151

Preface

Spiritual direction is both an ancient art and an evolving contemporary practice. The centuries-long tradition surrounding direction suggests its importance in advancing the spiritual lives of people in different historical periods. It has been a valuable and venerated process for countless serious believers. Yet there is also a contemporary quality to the practice of spiritual direction. In an age of specialization, spiritual direction has taken its rightful place as a specialized form of ministry which places particular demands on its practitioners. The emergence of training institutes for spiritual directors attests to the fact that spiritual direction is a demanding professional work with its own unique requirements.

People coming to direction today are from different age groups and from various walks of life, and they present specific challenges to directors. In responding to these people, directors have to relate their work to the concerns that are prominent at a certain life stage. Ongoing dialogue with specialists from other branches of ministry and from the secular helping professions can help focus the attention of directors on central issues which affect the spiritual development of people from each different age group.

It is my intent in this book to carry forward the dialogue between direction and other disciplines with reference to those at midlife. The midlife period has special relevance inasuch as a large number of people coming for spiritual direction are in that particular transition period. The goal of my bringing together the contributions of theologians, directors, psychologists and other professionals is to facilitate a more informed and effective response to midlife individuals in spiritual direction.

The term *midlife* is sometimes used to designate an age range as wide as thirty-five to fifty-five. However, the issues concerning the self, its limits, and a person's future potential are more crucial than chronological age for designating midlife. I suggest that with an increased awareness of these midlife issues directors can make more effective use of the Christian tradition in responding to and helping those in the midlife passage. Directors are required to be practical theologians helping individuals to interpret their experiences in the light of their religious heritage. This book is an exercise in practical theology inasmuch as it correlates the experience of people at midlife with Christian themes.

Throughout this book I have tried to remain faithful to the traditional teaching on direction while at the same time supporting refinements in practice on the basis of recent insights into spiritual growth and adult development. In working with those at midlife, spiritual directors need to be open to various approaches. For instance, some people with a director's assistance may profitably focus on images of self and God; others, however, need to move beyond images into the imageless realm of mystery. It is my hope that this book will help directors to meet the diverse needs of people at midlife.

During the writing of this book I have received support and encouragement from many friends and colleagues. I wish to express my gratitude to Drs. Paul W. Pruyser and John S. Homlish of the Menninger Foundation, whose interest in the work sustained me especially in the early stages of the project. Dr. Mary Cerney, O.S.F., also of the Menninger Foundation, and Louise Mary Smith offered assistance at critical stages in the book's evolution for which I am deeply grateful. I extend special thanks to Valerian Odermann, O.S.B., who made valuable suggestions for improving the text and Peter Ainslie who assisted in compiling the index. I also wish to acknowledge the support of my abbot, Timothy Sweeney, O.S.B., and members of the community of St. Meinrad Archabbey and of many colleagues and students in the School of Religious Studies of The Catholic University of America. Finally, I must thank those with whom I have had the privilege of sharing the experience of spiritual direction.

Raymond Studzinski, O.S.B.
The Catholic University of America
December, 1984

CHAPTER ONE

The Spiritual Challenge
of Midlife

In Graham Greene's novel, *A Burnt-Out Case*, a successful architect named Querry abandons his career and voyages deep into the African Congo.[1] He withdraws from people and becomes indifferent to life. While spending time with the staff of a leper colony at the farthest point of his journey, he is invited to reclaim his vocation as an architect by designing and overseeing the construction of a hospital. He responds: "When desire is dead one cannot continue to make love. I've come to the end of desire and to the end of a vocation. Don't try to bind me in a loveless marriage and to make me imitate what I used to perform with passion. And don't talk to me like a priest about my duty."[2]

A turning point in Querry's life comes when he tells the wife of a local factory manager a parable. Through that story Querry comes to terms with his own condition. He tells of a young man who grows up to be a successful jeweler and lover. However, the young man soon becomes disenchanted with his work, his loves, and the king he serves. The world, which for him has been a sea of objects to be manipulated for his own pleasure, now ceases to gratify him. Eventually he comes to doubt the very existence of the king about whom his parents have talked since he was a child. "There was left only a memory of the King who had lived in his parents' heart and not in any particular place. Unfortunately his heart was not the same as the one his parents shared: it was callused with pride and success. . . ."[3] Querry continues, "There were moments when he wondered if his unbelief were not after all a final and conclusive proof of the King's existence. This total vacancy might be his punishment for the rules he

1

had wilfully broken. It was even possible that this was what people meant by pain."[4]

The friend who listens attentively to the story does Querry a great service, for she enables him in the telling of the tale to discover an image of his own condition. It is the prelude to Querry's restoration as a human person, able once again to invest himself in life, vocation, and other people.

Greene's novel presents a paradigm of healing. Human beings alienated from themselves and other people can recover wholeness through storytelling, experiences of mystery, and moments of communion. The novel speaks to the experience of many people. In a dedicatory letter which prefaces the novel, Graham Greene says: "This is not a *roman à clef*, but an attempt to give dramatic expression to various types of belief, half-belief, and non-belief, in the kind of setting, removed from world-politics and household-preoccupations, where such differences are felt acutely and find expression. This Congo is a region of the mind. . . ."[5]

Querry's condition typifies an experience that some people have at midlife. They find they are disenchanted with themselves and with all that is going on around them. Many have the sense of having reached the limits of life at what is only its midpoint. Boredom is often their lot. Reactions to this experience vary greatly with individuals, but many feel the need to strike out in a new direction.

A whole body of literature, ranging from scientific studies to popular books and articles, has recently emerged which addresses itself to questions about midlife.[6] If the eager consumption of this material on adult development is any indication, the phenomenon of uncertainty and reappraisal at midlife is not rare. Many adults in their late thirties and in their forties and fifties are again raising issues resolved years earlier—and supposedly settled forever—and are searching for some direction in their midlife journey.

Confronted with personal finiteness and the inevitability of approaching death, many people are forced to reconsider how they understand themselves, what will make them happy, and what will give their lives continued meaning. For them midlife is the time when the past comes up for review and is re-evaluated so that they can arrive at more realistic expectations for the future. Some people handle midlife quietly and smoothly, others experience considerable

2

upheaval, indeed a "midlife crisis." For all, there is a "midlife transition," a process or change which marks this period in life.[7]

Midlife transitions affect people at all levels of society. Nor are they only a contemporary phenomenon. Literature from many different historical periods describes midlife confrontations with emptiness and meaninglessness.[8] In *Pilgrim's Progress*, Bunyan captures in classic form the anxiety of such an experience: ". . . he [the pilgrim] burst out, as he had done before, crying, 'What shall I do to be saved?' I saw also that he looked this way, and that way, as if he would run; yet he stood still, because, as I perceived, he could not tell which way to go."[9]

Bunyan's "pilgrim" is an individual in midlife who has set out on the painful course toward a greater degree of integration and fulfillment. The context in which he exerts himself, as in much similar literature, is a journey. One contemporary authority has commented on these novels of development in this way: "The mid-life journey, while it engages the hero in adventures demanding his participation, affects his inner comprehension of himself and his world. His journey is from the world of the established order of past experience, to other worlds not encountered beforehand, and, metaphorically, the journey to his center. Because the experience is conditioned by his particular history, the course he must follow is uncharted except by the responses of thought, desire, and affectivity he has developed."[10] Whereas the fictional presentation of such a journey usually makes for fascinating reading, the real experience of the midlife journey can be terrifying and humiliating. And yet, people find themselves making such journeys, and in the midst of their anguish they often wonder why.

This book is about a group of people who are in anguish over the stormy journey of midlife transition. They are those dedicated individuals within the churches today who have sincerely tried to use religious beliefs as a framework for their lives. They sometimes hold positions of leadership in society as well as in the church. Their situation is often made more difficult because they are held up as models of stability. When they experience internal upheaval in the middle of life, their first reaction is to disappear quietly from the scene in order to sort things out. Often, however, they feel constrained to stay with their current responsibilities. They may strive to

3

cover over the rupture which exists between what they do in a stable church and what they are thinking and feeling as persons who are suddenly adrift. But they can also set out on an interior journey to gain new perspectives on themselves and their work. On such a journey they will probably benefit from having a companion with whom they can share their inner experience, and from the sharing they will formulate new directions for their own future.

The search for a companion to assist in the midlife struggle leads to many possibilities. Some, wishing to keep their struggles to themselves, do not look for a companion but for a sourcebook to provide them with the information they feel they need. Their hope is that there is a *vade mecum* which will clarify their experience. Others will approach their struggles with the help of a professional person and seek out a psychotherapist or counselor. Still others will turn to a religious person who has helped them at other times and whom they regard as a spiritual director, a person who has helped to facilitate their growth.

Those who look to a spiritual director at midlife hope to gain a deeper spiritual and psychological insight into themselves, because they sense that their emotional turmoil is somehow related to their continuing religious development. Consequently, the spiritual director whom these people select must be sensitive to the spiritual and psychological issues of midlife. This book attempts to increase this sensitivity in spiritual directors and to suggest ways in which they can be most helpful to those who approach them for assistance at midlife.

Adequate preparation of spiritual directors for helping people in midlife is very important. This is especially true because spiritual directors may experience some role confusion when they are approached by people who are struggling with midlife problems. Some of these problems will strike directors as emotional difficulties. Directors may wonder whether they are being asked to function as psychotherapists or counselors. Indeed, there are cases when a referral of a troubled individual to a counselor or psychotherapist is in order, but at the same time directors should not underestimate the help they can give to fellow believers. While directors need to be clear on what spiritual direction is—its distinctive nature and scope—they also need to see it as clearly related to other helping processes like psychotherapy or counseling.

Spiritual Direction and Other Helping Processes

Spiritual direction, like all ministry in the Christian church, has its roots in the gospel.[11] The biblical accounts of the life and work of Jesus provide patterns for ministerial life and service. The Markan account of the rich man who approached Jesus with a question regarding salvation serves as a starting point for an understanding of spiritual direction:

> And as he was setting out on his journey, a man ran up and knelt before him, and asked, "Good Teacher, what must I do to inherit eternal life?" And Jesus said to him, "Why do you call me good? No one is good but God alone. You know the commandments: 'Do not kill, Do not commit adultery, Do not steal, Do not bear false witness, Do not defraud, Honor your father and mother.' " And he said to him, "Teacher, all these I have observed from my youth." And Jesus looking upon him loved him, and said to him, "You lack one thing; go, sell what you have, and give to the poor, and you will have treasure in heaven; and come, follow me." At that saying his countenance fell, and he went away sorrowful; for he had great possessions (Mk 10:17–22).[12]

Just as the man's question to Jesus was not trivial, so, too, the questions which midlife Christians raise in spiritual direction are serious and consequential. They are questions which come from the depth of a person's being. They spring from a deep concern that religious fidelity is not getting him or her anywhere or that it has not resulted in a sense of peace and integration. Spiritual direction is concerned with people who have come to an impasse in their life of faith. They seek out a spiritual director to help them understand what might be holding them back from a fuller life and to help them discover positive steps that they can take. These concerns are germane to the nature of spiritual direction, a process where one person helps another come to fuller maturity in the faith.[13]

The Markan account of the rich man also reveals other features of spiritual direction. There is no coercion involved in the process; it is a free activity for both director and the directee. "And he went away sorrowful; for he had great possessions." Jesus did not chase after him. Direction is a human encounter in which thoughts and feelings are shared. It is concerned with a person's life history, religious observance, life-style, and openness to God and other people. It appeals to the individual's yearning for the transcendent, for that

5

which lies beyond earthly existence, while it does not disregard earthly strivings and aspirations.

The term *spiritual direction* can lead to misunderstandings about the nature of the direction process. The word *spiritual* may give the impression that the process is involved with only one aspect of the person coming for direction. However, *spiritual* has its roots in Pauline anthropology, where the word refers to a human existence in which body, soul, and spirit are integrated into a unity. The final blessing in the First Letter to the Thessalonians reveals Paul's unified view of the human person: "May the God of peace himself sanctify you wholly; and may your spirit and soul and body be kept sound and blameless at the coming of our Lord Jesus Christ" (5:23).[14]

The use of the word *direction* can also be misleading. The process of spiritual direction does not involve one person telling another how to live and act. Direction for living and acting is not found in the advice of a director as in some prefabricated scheme, but in the fabric of the individual's life which is being brought into sharper focus through the facilitating efforts of the director. The directee discovers that God is in his or her life, guiding, sustaining, and leading to a fuller integration of self. While time is spent in discussing the directee's prayer and religious thought, the direction process is holistic, and no dimension of a person's life is irrelevant to it.[15]

Spiritual direction has much in common with other helping processes such as psychotherapy and counseling. Like counseling, spiritual direction may adopt a task-centered approach at times for the resolution of some particular difficulty. It differs from counseling inasmuch as the direction relationship continues even after immediate problems have been solved; for direction is concerned with the larger issues of continuing growth and development. Direction has benefited from the insights and techniques developed in the area of counseling, but it is often more concerned with the broader aspects of an individual's thought and feeling than counseling is.[16] Directors, for instance, often strive to enable persons to discover for themselves the larger motives guiding their lives, motives which are often not immediately apparent. Of course, directors and counselors look at the same reality; it is just that the director looks at an individual as one whose life is a continuum of religious and human growth. This life, if it is to be fully understood, calls for a sensitivity to the dynamics of belief and the challenges to faith development.[17]

Direction also bears many similarities to the psychotherapeutic process, since it is not indifferent to emotional difficulties and developmental arrests. In fact, it views these as concerns that are intimately related to the achievement of integration by the religiously oriented person. In an essay on integration Thomas Merton commented on the interrelationship of psychological health and religious growth: ". . . Let us make clear that ordinarily a full spiritual development and a supernatural, even charismatic, maturity, evidenced in the 'saint,' normally includes the idea of complete psychological integration. Doubtless many saints have been neurotics, but they have used their neurosis in the interests of growth instead of capitulating and succumbing to its dubious comforts."[18] The concern of the spiritual director is and should be the whole human person. The director quite legitimately pays attention to the interplay of spiritual and psychological dynamics within the life of an individual person.

Like psychotherapy, spiritual direction is interested in the life history, the thoughts, the feelings and the aspirations of an individual. Both disciplines also pay attention to personal relationships, those which persons have had with other people in their past as well as those which they currently have. Both disciplines are concerned with enabling persons to relate more maturely by coming to terms with problematic relationships in the past which may still have considerable influence in their lives. Psychotherapists approach clients with a special sensitivity to pathological conditions which may exist. They examine behavior in a search for symptoms that may suggest certain conflicts.

The goal of psychotherapy is to alleviate symptoms and correct any pathology so that, in Freud's phrase, a person may love and work well. Spiritual direction shares this goal but is carried out on the assumption that loving and working well is centrally connected with the relationship that a person has with God. In direction the focus is not on pathology but on normal conflict and on discovering and realizing one's potential for love and work in the service of God.[19] Kenneth Leech in *Soul Friend* sums up the relationship between the two disciplines in this way: "The aim of spiritual direction is the achievement of wholeness of life, an integrated personality, in which the inner and the outer man are united. Yet to become whole and integrated is painful, it is a process which involves conflict and crisis, and all spiritual direction is involved in the crises of the soul. The

7

death and resurrection experience is repeated in the life of the soul, and the context of this experience is the area where psychology and theology overlap. For both theologian and therapist are involved with the wholeness of man, with his inner world, and with the cure of souls."[20]

Both spiritual direction and psychotherapy depend for their effectiveness on the motivation of the person who comes for help. Both provide an objective reference point in the person of the director or therapist who enables the individual seeking help to see aspects o: self which otherwise he or she might not see. Yet psychotherapy is primarily oriented to the present and to the past which has led up to it. While not neglecting these, spiritual direction has a more transcendent orientation as it looks from the present to the future and even to a person's life beyond the grave. It seeks to discover in the life of the individual a unique plan whose source is God and which leads to full religious and human development through deliberate choices in the here and now.[21]

Furthermore, both spiritual direction and psychotherapy share a concern for the decision-making processes of the individual seeking help. The therapist attempts to bring the unconscious influences which govern a person's choices to consciousness in order to help a person control more effectively the various aspects of his or her life. Direction also attempts to make a person more aware of the diverse elements involved in decision making through a process called discernment. The exercise of discernment involves an assessment of inspirations, intuitions, and impulses in terms of their sources and their congruity with the overall direction of the person's religious life. Like the psychotherapeutic techniques, discernment results in a better knowledge of the self and the various influences which affect the self.

For people who are actively involved with God and the church, spiritual direction provides a unique forum where aspects of that involvement can be discussed. But spiritual direction does more than that. It also provides a forum for examining the central issues of life. Direction challenges a person to confront the demands of reality and to grow in faith as he or she deals with them maturely. It does not encourage escape or deception. In fact, the spiritual director helps people discover self-deceptions and helps them follow courses which lead to a full acceptance of the truth about themselves, about reality, and about God. This is accomplished, in part, by an honest appro-priation of one's past with all its ups and downs. Despite the negative features of any personal history, directees learn to find the action of God in their own histories. They come to believe in a deeply personal way that God is directing them into the future. This movement into the future involves greater fidelity to their true selves and a stronger relationship of service and love to the community of persons with whom they are involved.

Spiritual direction provides the opportunity for an in-depth exploration of a person's prayer, one's intimate relationship with God. Like any other relationship, this one has the possibility of evolving and becoming more mature or of stagnating and regressing to an immature level. A spiritual director is concerned about facilitat-ing a person's movement toward a deeper relationship with God. The director encourages persons to become more fully themselves before God. Through this openness before God, the God of Truth, persons come to an acceptance of all their feelings and especially their nega-tive or dark side. An impetus for this development is the individual's continuing discovery of God's personal and particular love for him or her, which the director strives to reflect by showing an acceptance for and love of the complete person. This experience of acceptance is health-producing; it fosters a healthier religious orientation and a healthier emotional life.

By actively pursuing a better prayer life, a person begins to purify his or her image of God. It is gradually stripped of projected and immature qualities. This can be a painful, depressing time. The direc-tor helps directees to weather this storm when they may feel aban-doned by God or even feel real hatred for God. Directors view such experiences developmentally, since they are aware that pain and conflict are inevitable in any movement toward a more fully inte-grated life. Rather than viewing the directee as rejecting his or her faith in these periods of turmoil, directors are sensitive to the growth in faith which takes place in the midst of the turmoil, and so they can encourage the directee to begin to make those adaptations which a starker conception of God and of reality may require. As old defen-sive maneuvers collapse, the director tries to encourage different adaptations whereby anxiety and suffering need not be denied or projected outward but can be honestly confronted and recognized as arising from the self.

9

This process does not happen all at once. Though its onset may be sudden and insidious, the process may last for years. It is unquestionably a challenge to directees. In meeting it they may discover strengths which they did not realize they possessed. But the challenge is shared by the directors as well. They, too, are forced to become aware of the inadequacy of past solutions and past approaches as they reach into themselves and take hold of a new resourcefulness. Directing persons who are undergoing such a process of purification and change requires directors to stretch their own emotional and intellectual capacities.

Theoretically, the process of purification and change can happen to people at various times in their lives. However, it is during the midlife transition that the upheaval connected with the process is frequently most dramatic. The direction of persons in midlife transition calls for considerable skill and understanding on the part of directors. Directors may feel that the personal cost for them is quite high. But if they choose to make the investment of their time and energy, they can be privileged witnesses to the spiritual and psychological maturation of persons at critical junctures of their lives. More than that, they can be significantly involved in that growth process.

Midlife and Spirituality

There is ample evidence to be found throughout the Christian spiritual tradition for periods of turmoil and change at the onset of midlife. Teresa of Avila at midlife left behind her settled way of life to embark on the career of a reformer. Her spirituality from that point on was an earnest quest for a closer union with God. Ignatius Loyola, in choosing for himself a life of service dedicated to God and the church, went through a midlife decision-making process which formed the basis for his *Spiritual Exercises*. For Teresa and Ignatius midlife held the promise of spiritual renewal. For some who have only had a minimal interest in God and religion, midlife can be a time of spiritual awakening in which they find new vitality and an increased meaning in life.

In a small section on spiritual crisis in her popular book *Passages*, Gail Sheehy concedes: "While religion yields less comfort to fewer people in this world of vanished certainties, it is a world view that has given many people a framework to make some sense out of the chaos."[22] She goes on to point out that midlife can also result in religious disillusionment. She uses the example of a forty-year-old minister looking for a way out of his confining religious position. "He was the one who was supposed to have all the answers, and he was not in touch with the answer machine. He wanted room to admit his own fallibility, his anger, his need to be stroked, and all his other blocked feelings. . . . [His] solution is to find his humanity by sharing his uncertainties with men and women, ministers, researchers, and writers, people like himself who seek a refreshment of purpose in midlife."[23] Though she gives only minimal attention to the religious questions of midlife, Sheehy suggests that midlife is often the occasion for a shift in religious orientation.

Other writers show a stronger interest in spiritual issues. Indeed, Carl Jung, a recognized pioneer in the study of midlife, has found that religious questioning was often a central dilemma in the midlife search of people he had treated. In *Modern Man in Search of a Soul,* Jung remarks: "Among all my patients in the second half of life—that is to say, over thirty-five—there has not been one whose problem in the last resort was not that of finding a religious outlook on life. It is safe to say that every one of them fell ill because he had lost that which the living religions of every age have given to their followers, and none of them has been really healed who did not regain his religious outlook."[24] Jung insisted on the desirability of psychotherapists and clergy working together to meet the spiritual crisis of modern times. He once sent a questionnaire out to friends in which he asked whom they would consult at a time of spiritual distress, a doctor or a clergyman. In the responses, the answer most often given for not choosing a clergyman was his lack of psychological knowledge and insight. Jung quotes an angry remark of one respondent: "Theology has nothing to do with the treatment of human beings."[25] This observation was made over fifty years ago; not a few people would agree with it today.

A poignant challenge to spiritual theology and spiritual direction is being expressed by many Christians at midlife who are leading Thoreau's "lives of quiet desperation." The failure to respond adequately to these people raises questions about the ability of theology to illuminate the human dilemma. Is spiritual suffering, soul-sickness, or the desire for something more in life irrelevant to theology? Religious people would readily say that it is not. But this

11

response raises the question of how theology can be brought to bear directly on the lives of believers.

Developmental psychology points in the right direction. To recognize that adult life is a continuous growth process is not new to theological thought, but contemporary psychological research can suggest ways of dealing with spiritual needs throughout the life course of an individual.[26] Religious people, in particular, may become frustrated at midlife by the apparent emptiness of theological concepts; even though the vision of life which these concepts conveyed has satisfied them for many years. Looking for a more dynamic understanding of theology, of Christian life, and of themselves, they are ready to take the next step in their faith development. The directors to whom these people go must likewise be ready and courageous enough to accompany them on the journey toward a deeper vision of life and be ready to assist at a birth which will involve labor pains for themselves as well.

The religious quest in the second half of life is not necessarily dramatic. It may simply be a quiet, interior pursuit. Reluctant to have their spiritual search visible to others and not wanting to unsettle others who have perceived them as stable in their faith practice, a person may only reveal his or her spiritual search to a trusted and respected individual. Even then the revelation may be somewhat oblique and may be conveyed only with a desire to establish a relationship with someone who seems to be at peace and who lives wisely. The revelation may occur in much the same way as when Nicodemus came to Jesus in his ministry.

> Now there was a man of the Pharisees, named Nicodemus, a ruler of the Jews. This man came to Jesus by night and said to him, "Rabbi, we know that you are a teacher come from God; for no one can do these signs that you do, unless God is with him." Jesus answered him, "Truly, truly, I say to you, unless one is born anew, he cannot see the kingdom of God." Nicodemus said to him, "How can a man be born when he is old? Can he enter a second time into his mother's womb and be born?" Jesus answered, "Truly, truly, I say to you, unless one is born of water and the Spirit, he cannot enter the kingdom of God. That which is born of the flesh is flesh, and that which is born of the Spirit is spirit. Do not marvel that I said to you, 'You must be born anew.' The wind blows where it wills, and you hear the sound of it, but you do not know whence it comes or whither it goes; so it is with every one who is born of the Spirit (Jn 3:1–8).

Nicodemus is understandably baffled by Jesus' suggestion that he must be born again. The human experience of conflict that occurs when one is leaving behind one way of life and embracing a new one is baffling. In Johannine literature the night symbolizes the forces of evil and the demonic power of the world. As Nicodemus begins his rite of passage by coming at night, the relationship with Jesus has a profound effect on him. He encounters Jesus and is illuminated by him. The human elements of fear and confusion are there, "Nicodemus said to him, 'How can this be?' Jesus answered him, 'Are you a teacher of Israel, and yet you do not understand this?' " (Jn 3:9–10).

In some ways the account of Nicodemus coming to Jesus makes a good analogy for the experience of a religious person coming to someone for spiritual direction. In metaphor, one can see the midlife Christian moving through his or her own darkness in an effort to gain some light. The elements of fear and confusion are there. Jesus challenged Nicodemus to be born again and to live in the light. "For every one who does evil hates the light, and does not come to the light, lest his deeds be exposed" (Jn 8:20). Jesus' words embody a call to conversion.

Being aware that conversion is a lifelong process, the director helps the Christian continue to respond to this call. Persons at midlife have responded to the call long ago. They may feel that they are being asked to retrace their steps in life. The movement into midlife does, in fact, present persons with opportunities to reexamine and modify many of their relationships and their thoughts about life, themselves, and God. The experience of a midlife passage resembles the movement to a deeper conversion. While religious terminology is not often used in contemporary literature about midlife, it does provide a good framework for a director's understanding of the tasks which are connected with psychological as well as spiritual growth. Conversely, the psychological literature suggests ways in which the director can perceive the life of faith on the developmental model. These ways will be taken up again in chapter 3.

Conversion

Recently Bernard Lonergan has written about the experience of conversion. Conversion at its richest is for Lonergan a radical transformation of a person that brings before him a world of new values.

13

"It is not merely a change or even a development; rather, it is a radical transformation on which follows, on all levels of living, an interlocked series of changes and developments. What hitherto was unnoticed becomes vivid and present. What had been of no concern becomes a matter of high import. So great a change in one's apprehensions and one's values accompanies no less a change in oneself, in one's relations to other persons, and in one's relations to God."[27] Conversion, of course, is not always at such a high level of intensity, as Lonergan admits. What is constant is the change of orientation, the movement toward greater openness to the truth, to the good, and ultimately to God. Accordingly, Lonergan specifies three types of conversion—intellectual, moral, and religious. Each of these involves the giving up of long-held ideas and practices in order to embrace life more completely.

To part with the past is, of course, a painful, wrenching process. The pain connected with conversion often reaches overpowering proportions at midlife. Even for religious people who may have grown accustomed to ongoing conversion, the call for a still more radical change of heart is dismaying. Thomas Merton wrote: "We are not converted only once in our lives, but many times, and this endless series of large and small conversions, inner revolutions, leads to our transformation in Christ. But, while we may have the generosity to undergo one or two such upheavals, we cannot face the necessity of further and greater rendings of our inner self, without which we cannot finally become free."[28] Conversion at midlife frequently invites persons to leave behind some of their most cherished assumptions, especially the assumption that they are in charge of their lives. In short, persons at midlife may feel as though they are being asked to surrender their freedom.

In a penetrating essay dealing with conversion in the second half of life, David Burrell relates the thoughts of Carl Jung on changed goals and relationships in midlife to the rules drawn up by St. John of the Cross for progress in the spiritual life. According to Burrell's synthesis, the transition from *doing* to *suffering* is central to conversion in the second half of life. Whereas formerly individuals had chosen their life projects, their relationships, even their relations to God to a certain extent, they now *suffer* the choices they have made. "Suffering of this sort is not necessarily connected with pain—unless it be the painful state of not being in charge. But *that* suffering cannot be

14

anything but salutary—for the world as well as for me. For even if I could take charge of my life, I wouldn't; my demons would."[29] Burrell goes on to suggest that this shift from doing to undergoing constitutes the real passage to adulthood and it occurs in the second half of life. To let this shift happen is to undergo a death. The death brings with it an end to the bondage which people create for themselves to the demons of idealized power, self-sufficiency, and the ambition to get ahead. In the language of John of the Cross, "Freedom cannot abide in a heart dominated by the appetites—in a slave's heart; it dwells in a liberated heart which is a son's heart."[30] The process of liberation, begun at the outset of midlife, is carried out as a response to the Lord's continuing call to conversion. Prayer itself becomes purified of cloying self-interest and more authentically Other-directed. Self-projects of all sorts are surrendered so that one's determining task in life becomes the upbuilding of the community which the person serves.

The Dark Night

Midlife conversion entails considerable losses. People seldom realize how centered their lives are on ideals of getting ahead or acquiring power until they gradually try to remove these from their lives. The loss of these ideals is disorienting and confusing as Dante recounts in the *Inferno* of *The Divine Comedy*:

> In the middle of the journey of our life
> I came to myself within a dark wood
> Where the straight way was lost.[31]

Dante suggests other images which are frequently used with reference to the experience of a religious midlife transition—darkness and the journey. The "dark night" of John of the Cross has become a catch phrase to describe a period of depression in which there is loneliness and a crisis about the goals and the meaning of life. Night is an apt expression for this period not only because it captures the negative aspects of being enveloped in darkness, but also because it hints at some of the positive features of the experience as well.

Edith Stein in her study of John of the Cross has presented a phenomenological description of the experience of a dark night. The dark night falls over people; it is formless and invisible; it swallows them and everything around them. They experience a sense of being

15

paralyzed, as well as blindness. The night is threatening. It presents people with a foretaste of death. The dark night affects them both inwardly and outwardly. Yet this same night has a comforting side. "It ends the noise and bustle of the day; it brings peace and quiet. All this also has its effects in the psychological and spiritual spheres. There is a nocturnal, gentle transparence of the spirit freed from the busy-ness of the day, relaxed but also collected, so that it can be drawn into the profound relationships of its own being and life, in the natural and supernatural worlds. And there is a deep and grateful repose in the peace of the night."[32] John of the Cross also noted these positive aspects:

> On a night of darkness,
> In love's anxiety of longing kindled,
> O Blessed chance!
> I left by none beheld,
> My house in sleep and silence stilled.

> • • •

> By dark of blessed night,
> In secrecy, for no one saw me
> And I regarded nothing,
> My only light and guide
> The one that in my heart was burning.[33]

The dark night for John of the Cross is, above all, a time of faith. In the darkness a person learns to believe that God is present despite feelings to the contrary. This is purified faith, a faith that is functioning in circumstances which would seem to frustrate believing. It is a solitary faith, for in the darkness a person experiences aloneness. Yet it is a unifying faith, for the person is required to gather the self together, as it were, in making this act of faith. All the energy a person has is drawn together and concentrated in this act of going out of the self and placing one's trust in an unseen and unexperienced God.

The result of all this is a paradoxical personal centering and integration. As God becomes the center of one's life and existence, a person senses that he or she has become more aware of his or her true self. The darkness has enabled the person to make an important discovery about the self and its relationship to God. The discovery is liberating. Self-preoccupations which may have weighed on a person

16

can now be set aside. Issues which have been avoided can now be faced. Even death, which previously caused terror in one's sense of self, can now be looked at objectively. Such experience resonates with the vibrant revelation contained in the Scriptures. "I am the light of the world; he who follows me will not walk in darkness, but will have the light of life. If you continue in my word, you are truly my disciples, and you will know the truth, and the truth will make you free" (Jn 8:12, 31–32).

The Journey

The most common image used for any religious transition is that of a journey. The journey metaphor is used by John of the Cross throughout his writings. In *The Ascent of Mount Carmel* he speaks of the interior journey as a movement of the soul through gradual purifications to a closer union with God.[34] In our age of easy travel, people may have to be reminded of the difficulty involved in making a journey in ages past. It meant exposing oneself to all kinds of dangers. It took long periods of time, sometimes years. The circumstances surrounding a journey made it an apt image for expressing the experience of a midlife transition. One left one's homeland and risked life and fortune to reach another place, not because that place was better than the homeland, but because one felt an interior call to make the journey.

Mark Searle has brought together the images we have discussed here in an article entitled "The Journey of Conversion."[35] He speaks about the current interest in midlife as an opportunity for people to rediscover within the Christian tradition the fundamental theme of movement or transition in the Christian life. He sees the journey of conversion as a movement through crisis to a fuller experience of life. He defines crisis broadly as a turning point or moment of change. Following the rough outline of any story, Searle discusses the journey of conversion in terms of a setting out, an adventure, and a return. While the setting out on the journey may be precipitated by some significant event; this is not always the case. There may simply be a growing dissatisfaction with one's life in the way it is unfolding. This then produces the turning point which Searle speaks about. "It is a fact that we do not choose crisis: it is thrust upon us. No one sets out deliberately on a journey of conversion; he is always called to it, perhaps we had better say launched upon it, by circumstances outside his control. However we may react or try to cope, the kind of change which provokes crisis and calls us to conversion always comes at a time and in a manner not of our choosing. It is given, not chosen."[36]

The journey of conversion affects the whole person. The sum total of these effects drives one to use symbols to express what is happening. The adventure is extremely demanding, "Whatever name we give it, and however we might imagine it ourselves, it is a time of darkness and disorientation, occasionally a period of wild exhiliration, but always a time in which we seem to have broken our moorings, a time in which life appears to have spun out of control."[37] It is an encounter with death. It gives rise to a grieving process which, if allowed to run its course, culminates in acceptance and surrender. It is at this point that one can finally speak of a return. "Unexpectedly, one becomes aware that a new vision has been given, a relation has been granted, the grace of self transcendence, of new life, of joy. It is not that anything has necessarily changed. The loss or change which provoked the crisis have not been repealed, but we ourselves have been transformed and see it all anew."[38]

What seems to happen in these midlife conversion experiences is that one eventually penetrates through all the surface features of life to the very ground of one's being. There is an experience of being centered on that which truly endures, a sense of having found a center in God. The sense of self then seems solidly founded, and with this comes greater resilience and a deeper integration. The way to this stronger state has required giving up numerous fantasies about oneself and the world, but a new relationship with reality is established. Old dependencies become unnecessary and a radical dependence on God as the source of life and of the future is strengthened. Coupled with this is an awareness of what it means to be a creature wrought by God's hand. All this can come about if the turning point in an individual's life leads to a successful conversion process. Such is not always the case, as Searle points out. Fear can gain the upper hand and prevent a person from using a crisis as the entrance way to a deep conversion. The *status quo* can seem to be much more comfortable simply because it is familiar.[39]

Gerald O'Collins uses the concept of a "second journey" for a movement toward self discovery in the middle years, and he warns of "counterfeit destinations."[40] Enduring loneliness and apparent meaninglessness can wear a person down to the point where he or she is ready to settle for anything and cut the journey short. In an anxious desire to be freed of present commitments and without working through the various internal aspects of the struggle, a person may simply choose to escape to another place and gain nothing in self-understanding. O'Collins talks of the need for a careful discernment process if a person is to make the right choice. Like the chosen people longing for the fleshpots of Egypt, a person may hanker for a previous way of life, even a return to childhood, in the hope that all will be blissful again. In other words, there is a real danger of backsliding during these times of transition.[41] The pressure of change can bring out the best, but it can also bring out the worst in people.

O'Collins sees life as comprised of three journeys. The first journey is the passage out of childhood and adolescence into adulthood. The third one is the final movement toward death at the end of one's life. The second journey happens somewhere in between, though O'Collins is reluctant to associate it with any particular decade in the adult years. Nor does he hold that everyone follows this pattern. There are some, the "smooth evolvers," whose lives do not have any period which could clearly be designated a second journey. There are others in whose lives the three journeys merge so closely that it might be better to speak of the whole as a multifaceted move out of adolescence and into adulthood.[42] O'Collins does not see any essential differences in the second journeys of people in different walks of life. Of course, dedicated Christians, whatever their vocations, strive to understand what is happening to them in the light of the life and message of Jesus.

A time in the life of Jesus which can be paradigmatic for the Christian in midlife passage is the desert experience at the beginning of his public ministry. Prior to this experience, Jesus had received the baptism of repentance from John. He was then led by the Spirit into the desert, where he was put to the test. Matthew and Luke present three temptations to which Jesus was subject. Each temptation presented Jesus with a possible shortcut to the accomplishment of his mission. He could miraculously feed himself and the world by changing stones into bread. He could gain total political power and so claim the world for his Father. He could in a spectacular fashion show himself to be the favored one of God, endowed with faith in the

Father, and thus draw people to God. Filled with new insights into his identity, Jesus discerned that none of these three ways was the way he should walk; and he decisively chose the way of human servanthood. He took the longer and more difficult route of letting his mission shape his life, rather than his shaping the mission by the exercise of control over nature, nations, or even his Father.[43] He chose to walk the way of humanity, a way on which conflict would not be absent. "For we have not a high priest who is unable to sympathize with our weaknesses, but one who in every respect has been tempted as we are, yet without sin" (Heb 4:15).

Conflict awaits the individuals who strive in the depths of their being to recognize themselves as creatures of God and yet as persons in whom God has chosen to dwell. An ordinary level of self-consciousness is present in one's day-to-day activities. Those aspects of self which would interfere with this everyday activity are kept out of conscious awareness. The price we pay for this is that we are most familiar with only a part of ourselves. Anyone's self-definition is only partial. The task each person has as he or she journeys to a fuller life is to accept more and more of oneself, even the less attractive features which one would prefer to keep out of awareness.

This movement toward a fuller acceptance of one's whole self is one step along the way to a closer relationship with God. William Johnston has described this movement as something to be expected for those who are called to experience God more deeply in mystical prayer. "In the mystical life one passes from one layer to the next in an inner or downward journey to the core of the personality where dwells the great mystery called God—God who cannot be known directly, cannot be seen (for no man has ever seen God) and who dwells in thick darkness. This is the never-ending journey which is recognizable in the mysticism of all the great religions. It is a journey towards union because the consciousness gradually expands and integrates data from the so-called unconscious while the whole personality is absorbed into the great mystery of God."[44]

This confrontation with the darker side of oneself can be the occasion for a greater integration and an overcoming of the divisions which exist inside of a person. To accept the diverse tendencies within oneself can be a frightening and overwhelming experience. People find themselves profoundly unsettled and desperately wanting to cling to their former visions of themselves. As Johnston has written,

20

". . . great storms do arise and they can shake us to the roots of our being. One can be almost overwhelmed by gusts of anger or by nameless anxiety and fear, or by tumultuous sexuality, or by fierce rebellion against God and man. If a person has any neurotic tendencies . . . this is the time when they will clamour for fulfilment. This may be the time when, precisely because of the inner turmoil, one loses friends or fails in one's work or does something so utterly stupid that one looks like an idiot in the eyes of all."[45] This experience of turbulence and conflict may last for years and leave a person bereft. The Christian hope is that perseverance through these difficult times will bring a person to a more integrated level of existence. "When a woman is in travail she has sorrow, because her hour has come; but when she is delivered of the child, she no longer remembers the anguish, for joy that a child is born into the world" (Jn 16:21).

The story of a transition such as we have described is a story of death and rebirth. The old dies with a struggle; the new can only be adjusted to and approached with courage. Mourning the past and accepting the future are parts of the learning process of life. People want to speed up the process; people also want help in negotiating the various stages which they find themselves going through. In his writing on the stages of life, Carl Jung lamented that there were no colleges to prepare people for the second half of life; but then he proceeded to correct himself with the following observation: "I said just now that we have no schools for forty-year-olds. That is not quite true. Our religions were always such schools in the past, but how many people regard them as such today? How many of us older people have really been brought up in such a school and prepared for the second half of life, for old age, death and eternity?"[46]

Jung's question presents a challenge to religious people to make better use of the resources they have within religion itself. The challenge is to recognize that they live in a community of faith which has a rich tradition, a tradition which is still being lived out by people who are trying to relate their experiences to the testimony of countless Christians who have gone before them in the faith. While each journey in faith is unique in many ways, the general contours of these journeys are mapped out in the works of the spiritual masters. And "travelers" even today can find Christian people whose charism of the word is to help others achieve a better perspective on the vicissitudes of life.

21

After describing the conflict in which people of faith may find themselves, Johnston comments, "Happy the person who in this situation finds a sympathetic friend who will encourage and console and help him to understand the situation and see what is happening."[47] Such, of course, has been the good fortune of many Christians throughout history. The classic story of such an experience of blessing in the midst of confusion is told in the Gospel of Luke. It is the story of the two disciples on the way to Emmaus and their encounter with the Lord. " 'O foolish men, and slow of heart to believe all that the prophets have spoken! Was it not necessary that the Christ should suffer these things and enter into his glory?' And beginning with Moses and all the prophets, he interpreted to them in all the scriptures the things concerning himself" (Lk 24:25–27). In coming to understand what had happened to Jesus, these disciples were presented with a way to understand their own lives as well. The Lord came to them in their confusion and fear; he did not absent himself from their experience of conflict. They met him on the way, and his words effected an openness of spirit in them which led to their offer of hospitality. They gave thanks with him—perhaps even for the confusion and doubt which occasioned their coming to know him. He had broken the bread of God's word for them, and now he broke the bread of thanksgiving. "For he has not despised or abhorred the affliction of the afflicted; and he has not hid his face from him, but has heard when he cried to him" (Ps 22:24).

The Christian Paradigm

The pattern of the dying and rising of Jesus gives hope and meaning to every Christian life. For Jesus' followers the way to victory is the way of the cross; the way to life is the acceptance of death. The letting-go of what is precious to a person takes place not only at the end of life but also in the many small deaths which are part of human growth. Things are left behind so that a person can free himself to embrace the new. "When I was a child, I spoke like a child, I thought like a child, I reasoned like a child; when I became a man, I gave up childish ways" (1 Cor 13:11). Although Paul's words may suggest that the surrender of childish ways is a once-for-all occurrence, experience tells us that the childish is not easily or quickly surrendered. One works at this surrender throughout a lifetime. A person must even struggle to leave behind his or her childish notions of God. The experience is painful; and every person can appropriate the words of the psalmist about being forsaken by God. It is Jesus who, as the pioneer of salvation, is the model of steadfast faith in the face of desolation. "For because he himself has suffered and been tempted, he is able to help those who are tempted" (Heb 2:18).

The experience of God's distance or absence which occurs at midlife may come as a painful blow to the Christian. Just when the end of human life comes more into consciousness, God as the buffer for human fear seems to be gone. The experience can seem like a taste of hell. Dante's words at the age of thirty-seven seem apropos: "Ah, how hard it is to tell of that wood, savage and harsh and dense, the thought of which renews my fear! So bitter is it that death is hardly more."[48] In a reflection on the creedal statement "He descended into Hell," Karl Rahner points out how the experience of Jesus makes what is dreadful in people's lives bearable. "Since he has descended into the unfathomable and bottomless depths of the world, there is no longer any abyss in human experience in which man is abandoned and alone. There is one who has gone before him and has endured all such abysses, so that we might conquer. Henceforward whatever disasters may befall, at the bottom of them all is to be found eternal life."[49]

Faith as the commitment of one's whole self to the Living God can reach a new level of intensity as people at midlife confront the reality of their own death. The way to this deeper faith is again the way of the cross. The cross is the Christian symbol of life coming through death and of light coming through darkness. As Jesus surrendered his life on the cross, "the curtain of the temple was torn in two, from top to bottom" (Mk 15:38), an event which signifies for Christians the unhindered entrance into God's presence, an entrance which was accomplished by Jesus' death. Faith in what has been accomplished in Jesus leads Christians to accept the cross and ultimately to accept the removal of the curtains which were erected in their childish pasts to contain and confine the presence of God. God is no longer confined; he is to be found in all human experience. "He who descended is he who also ascended far above all heavens, that he might fill all things. And his gifts were that some should be apostles, some prophets, some evangelists, some pastors and teachers, to equip the saints for the work of ministry, for building up the body of Christ, until we all attain to the unity of the faith and of the knowledge of the Son of God, to mature manhood, to the measure of the stature of the fulness of Christ" (Eph 4:10–13).

Notes to Chapter One

1. (New York: Viking Press, 1961). This section follows the analysis of features of this novel in Wesley A. Kort, *Narrative Elements and Religious Meaning* (Philadelphia: Fortress Press, 1975), pp. 46–48.

2. Greene, p. 57.

3. *Ibid.*, pp. 196–97.

4. *Ibid.*, p. 197.

5. *Ibid.*, p. vii.

6. The following are a sampling: Janice Brewi and Anne Brennan, *Mid-Life: Psychological and Spiritual Perspectives* (New York: Crossroad, 1982); O. C. Brim, "Theories of the Male Mid-Life Crisis," *The Counseling Psychologist*, 6 (1976), 2–9; James Conway, *Men in Midlife Crisis* (Elgin, Ill.: Cook, 1978); Elliott Jaques, "The Midlife Crisis," in *The Course of Life: Psychoanalytic Contributions Toward Understanding Personality Development*, Vol. III, *Adulthood and the Aging Process*, ed. by Stanley I. Greenspan and George H. Pollock (Washington, D.C.: US Government Printing Office, 1980), pp. 1–23; Michael E. McGill, *The 40- to 60-Year Old Male: A Guide for Men—and the Women in Their Lives—To See Them Through the Crisis of the Male Middle Years* (New York: Simon and Schuster, 1980); Nancy Meyer, *The Male Mid-Life Crisis* (New York: Viking Press, 1978); K. Mogul, "Women in Midlife: Decisions, Rewards and Conflicts Related to Work and Careers," *American Journal of Psychiatry*, 136 (1979), 1139–43; Sheila Murphy, "Women's Midlife Mourning: The Wake of Youth," *Human Development*, 2 (1981), 21–26; William H. Norman and Thomas J. Scaramella, eds., *Mid-Life: Developmental and Clinical Issues* (New York: Brunner/Mazel, 1980); M. Notman, "Midlife Concerns of Women: Implications of the Menopause," *American Journal of Psychiatry*, 136 (1979), 1270–74; Kenn Rogers, "The Mid-Career Crisis," *Saturday Review of Society*, 1 (1973), 37–38; Lillian Rubin, *Women of a Certain Age: The Midlife Search for Self* (New York: Harper & Row, 1979); Sean D. Sammon, "Life After Youth: The Midlife Transition and Its Aftermath," *Human Development*, 3 (1982), 15–25; and James R. Zullo, "The Crisis of Limits: Midlife Beginnings," *Human Development*, 3 (1982), 6–14.

7. See the discussion of terminology in Calvin A. Colarusso and Robert A. Nemiroff, *Adult Development: A New Dimension in Psychodynamic Theory and Practice* (New York and London: Plenum Press, 1981), p. 121.

8. See Bridget Puzon, "The *Bildungsroman* of Middle Life," *Harvard Library Bulletin*, 26 (1978), 77.

9. John Bunyan, *The Pilgrim's Progress from This World to That Which Is to Come*, 2nd ed., ed. by James B. Wharey and Roger Sharrock (Oxford: Oxford University Press, 1967), p. 9.

10. Puzon, p. 5; see also her "The Hidden Meaning in *Humphrey Clinker*," *Harvard Library Bulletin*, 24 (1976), 40–54.

11. The core scriptural concept which underlies the ministry of spiritual direction is discernment. Although the gospels do not use the term, they

present Jesus as the discerner of the Father's will and the disciples as slowly discerning God as present and active in Jesus. See Jacques Guillet *et al.*, *Discernment of Spirits*, trans. by Innocentia Richards (Collegeville, Minn.: The Liturgical Press, 1970). For the early history and development of spiritual direction, see "Direction Spirituelle," *Dictionnaire de Spiritualité Ascetique et Mystique*, III (Paris: Beauschesne, 1957), cc. 1002–1214.

12. All scriptural quotations are taken from the Revised Standard Version of the Bible.

13. On the general nature of spiritual direction see the following: William A. Barry and William J. Connolly, *The Practice of Spiritual Direction* (New York: Seabury, 1982); William J. Connolly, "Contemporary Spiritual Direction: Scope and Principles: An Introductory Essay," *Studies in the Spirituality of Jesuits*, 7 (1975), 95–124; Katherine Marie Dyckman and L. Patrick Carroll, *Inviting the Mystic, Supporting the Prophet: An Introduction to Spiritual Direction* (New York: Paulist, 1981); Tilden Edwards, *Spiritual Friend* (New York: Paulist, 1980); David L. Fleming, "Models of Spiritual Direction," *Review for Religious*, 34 (1975), 351–57; Carolyn Gratton, *Guidelines for Spiritual Direction* (Denville, N.J.: Dimension Books, 1980); Damien Isabell, *The Spiritual Director: A Practical Guide* (Chicago: Franciscan Herald Press, 1975); Alan Jones, *Exploring Spiritual Direction: An Essay on Christian Friendship* (New York: Seabury, 1982); Morton T. Kelsey, *Companions on the Inner Way: The Art of Spiritual Guidance* (New York: Crossroad, 1983); Jean Laplace, *Preparing for Spiritual Direction*, trans. by John C. Guinness (Chicago: Franciscan Herald Press, 1975); Thomas Merton, *Spiritual Direction and Meditation* (Collegeville, Minn.: The Liturgical Press, 1960); Sandra M. Schneiders, *Spiritual Direction: Reflections on a Contemporary Ministry* (Chicago: National Sisters Vocation Conference, 1977); and Francis W. Vanderwall, *Spiritual Direction: An Invitation to Abundant Life* (New York: Paulist, 1981).

14. See Gratton, pp. 157–58.

15. See Sandra M. Schneiders for a discussion of the problem with the term "spiritual direction" in her essay "The Contemporary Ministry of Spiritual Direction," *Chicago Studies*, 15 (1976), 122–24; and also Gerald G. May, *Care of Mind/Care of Spirit: Psychiatric Dimensions of Spiritual Direction* (San Francisco: Harper & Row, 1982), pp. 7–8.

16. Kenneth Leech in his *Soul Friend: A Study of Spirituality* (London: Sheldon Press, 1977) delineates the relationship of spiritual direction to pastoral counseling and therapy; see Chapter 3, "Direction, Counselling and Therapy," pp. 90–136; see also May, pp. 12–17.

17. Leech, pp. 99–104.

18. Thomas Merton, "Final Integration: Toward a Monastic Therapy," in *Contemplation in a World of Action* (Garden City, N.Y.: Image Books, 1973), pp. 224–25.

19. Ruth Tiffany Barnhouse, "Spiritual Direction and Psychotherapy," *Journal of Pastoral Care*, 33 (1979), 149–63. Barnhouse comments on the different standards for judging results in psychotherapy and spiritual direction:

"Most psychotherapy measures results primarily against the needs and wishes of the individual, with varying amounts of consideration being given to the social requirements of the immediate community of which the subject forms a part. In short, the reference point is on the human social plane. By contrast, the reference point in spiritual direction is not on the human plane, but is the subject's relation to God, and the participation in the entire Christian community, the Invisible Body of Christ" (pp. 152–53). Barnhouse's essay has served as a guide for this section on the similarities and differences of spiritual direction and therapy.

20. Leech, pp. 108–09.

21. See John English, *Choosing Life* (New York: Paulist, 1978); Adrian van Kaam, *In Search of Spiritual Identity* (Denville, N.J.: Dimension Books, 1975), esp. pp. 249–59; and *idem, The Dynamics of Spiritual Self Direction* (Denville, N.J.: Dimension Books, 1976), esp. pp. 9–41.

22. *Passages: Predictable Crises of Adult Life* (New York: Bantam Books, 1976), p. 372.

23. *Ibid.*, pp. 372–74.

24. Trans. by W. A. Dell and Cary F. Baynes (New York: Harcourt, Brace & World, 1933), p. 229.

25. *Ibid.*, p. 230.

26. See William G. McCready, "Religion and the Life Cycle," in *Toward Vatican III: The Work That Needs To Be Done*, ed. by David Tracy with Hans Küng and Johann B. Metz (New York: Seabury, 1978), pp. 272–87; and Evelyn Eaton Whitehead and James D. Whitehead, *Christian Life Patterns: The Psychological Challenges and Religious Invitations of Adult Life* (Garden City, N.Y.: Doubleday, 1979).

27. Bernard Lonergan, "Theology in Its New Context," in *A Second Collection*, ed. by William F. J. Ryan and Bernard J. Tyrrell (London: Darton, Longman & Todd, 1974), pp. 65–66; see also *idem, Method in Theology* (New York: Herder and Herder, 1972); and B. C. Butler, "Bernard Lonergan and Conversion," *Worship*, 49 (1975), 329–336. Robert Doran has complemented Lonergan's treatment of conversion with a discussion of psychic conversion; see Doran's "Psychic Conversion," *The Thomist*, 41 (1977), 200–36.

28. Letter published in *Informations Catholiques Internationales* (April 1973), quoted by J. Pasquier, "Experience and Conversion," *The Way*, 17 (1977), 121.

29. David B. Burrell, "The Church and Individual Life," in *Toward Vatican III*, p. 126.

30. *The Collected Works of St. John of the Cross*, ed. by K. Kavanaugh and O. Rodriguez (Washington, D.C.: ICS Publications, 1973), p. 80.

31. *The Divine Comedy of Dante Alighieri*, I: *Inferno*, trans. by John D. Sinclair (New York: Oxford University Press, 1939), p. 23.

32. Edith Stein, *The Science of the Cross*, trans. by Hilda Graef (Chicago: H. Regnery, 1960), p. 26; see Gerald May's carefully nuanced discussion of the

differences between the "dark night" experience and clinical depression in *Care of Mind/Care of Spirit*, pp. 84–92. May notes: "To be fully accurate, one should probably not call the dark night an "experience" at all. It is more a deep and ongoing process of unknowing that involves the loss of habitual experience. This includes, at different times and in different ways, loss of attachment to sensate gratification and to usual aspirations and motivations, loss of previously construed faith-understandings, and loss of God-images. Accompanying this, of course, are loss of self-image/importance and of pre-conceptions about one's own identity" (p. 88).

33. Gerald Brenan, *St. John of the Cross: His Life and Poetry*, with a translation of his poetry by Lynda Nicholson (Cambridge: Cambridge University Press, 1975), p. 145.

34. *The Collected Works of St. John of the Cross*, pp. 81–83.

35. *Worship*, 54 (1980), pp. 35–55.

36. *Ibid.*, p. 38.

37. *Ibid.*, p. 39.

38. *Ibid.*, p. 43.

39. *Ibid.*, p. 44.

40. *The Second Journey* (New York: Paulist, 1978), pp. 67–70.

41. *Ibid.*, p. 69–70.

42. *Ibid.*, p. 75–76.

43. See G. B. Caird, *The Gospel of St. Luke*, The Pelican New Testament Commentaries (Baltimore: Penguin Books, 1963), pp. 79–81; and John C. Haughey, *The Conspiracy of God: The Holy Spirit in Men* (Garden City, N.Y.: Doubleday, 1973) pp. 33–39.

44. *The Inner Eye of Love: Mysticism and Religion* (San Francisco: Harper & Row, 1978), p. 127.

45. *Ibid.*, p. 129.

46. Jung, p. 109.

47. Johnston, p. 129.

48. *The Divine Comedy of Dante Alighieri*, I: *Inferno*, p. 23.

49. *Theological Investigations*, VII: *Further Theology of the Spiritual Life I*, trans. by David Bourke (New York: Herder and Herder, 1971), p. 150.

CHAPTER TWO

Psychic Integration and Midlife

Much of people's energy in the first half of life is spent in trying to "make it." This seems to be true in both the secular and the religious arenas. Settling on a vocation, finishing professional preparation, or finding one's niche in society and the church—all these contribute to a feeling of having arrived, of having left childhood behind, and of having become an adult. Maturity or adulthood is often assessed in terms of a person's arrival at a finished state. Yet adulthood, properly understood, always has an unfinished quality about it. It is a dynamic period when both the unresolved issues of childhood are worked on and new issues are faced; and both of these together call forth a greater maturity and a higher level of integration. Like childhood, adulthood has its own developmental tasks and challenges. How one meets these tasks and challenges affects every person's psychic equilibrium. Psychological develoment is not a fait accompli of childhood; its tasks continue throughout the adult years.

Adult Development

In the past few decades psychologists have become increasingly interested in the diverse aspects of adult development. Carl Jung (1875–1961) triggered interest in this area by recognizing the potential for further growth in life's second half. Jung found midlife to be a time of psychic revolution which can lead to a major shift in values as well as to the adoption of a new life program. Jung placed the "noon" of life sometime between the thirty-fifth and fortieth year, for around that time a person begins to experience a gradual decline in bodily vigor and a paling of youthful ambitions. Deep concerns about the self surface, and they begin to displace purely external preoccupations. This more introspective context often initiates a process of individuation which can bring about a profound sense of self-fulfillment.[1] These elements in Jung's pioneer work on midlife have been picked up and developed by several contemporary theorists.

One of the most influential thinkers on the developing human life cycle is Erik Erikson. Erikson has formulated a theory of the life course which consists of eight stages, each one associated with an important developmental task.[2] Six of these stages are found within the first half of life; the last of the six is the struggle for intimacy versus the tendency toward isolation. While the starting point for Erikson's work is Freudian psychoanalytic theory, he is more sensitive than Freud to the social matrix within which a person acts. For Erikson, psychological development follows a sequence of steps which are determined in part by increasing social relationships. Erikson expresses the matter this way: "Personality can be said to develop according to steps predetermined in the human organisms's readiness to be driven toward, to be aware of, and to interact with, a widening social radius, beginning with the dim image of a mother and ending with mankind, or at any rate that segment of mankind which 'counts' in the particular individual's life."[3]

In the middle and later years of life, Erikson posits only two stages. The first of these is the struggle for generativity over against self-absorption. This is followed by efforts to arrive at a sense of integrity rather than despair as the major part of a person's life stands revealed before him or her. There are considerable nuances to Erikson's presentation which are often overlooked by the commentators and theoreticians who claim dependence on him. Work on each of the developmental tasks continues throughout a person's life course, even though their attention shifts to the newest stage which they are entering. Erikson's study testifies to the largely unfinished nature of human development. "The idea that at any stage a *goodness* is achieved which is impervious to new conflicts within and changes without is a projection on child development of that success ideology which so dangerously pervades our private and public daydreams and can make us inept in the face of a heightened struggle for a meaningful existence in our time."[4]

George Vaillant has examined the movement through Erikson's

sequential (yet overlapping) stages in his work on the Grant Study, a longitudinal research project on men from the time they were freshmen at Harvard until they were in their fifties. The subjects chosen for the Grant Study were people who were thought to have the most promise. Vaillant has presented the results of his research on ninety-five of these men in his book *Adaptation to Life*.[5] He found Erikson's paradigm helpful. In their childhood these men negotiated the early stages and arrived at various degrees of basic trust, autonomy, initiative, and industry. As adolescents they strove to acquire an identity of their own. With the onset of the adult years, they worked on the establishment of intimacy.

Vaillant modifies Erikson's framework somewhat by inserting a stage called "career consolidation" between the stage leading to intimacy and that leading to generativity. He also adds a stage called "keeping the meaning" between the struggles for generativity and those for integrity.[6] Vaillant has pointed out, however, that while stage theory fits very well with child development, it is less appropriate for describing adult development. Certainly in these periods of adult development, the word *stage* has to be understood metaphorically.[7] For Vaillant, adult development does not happen so much in a stepwise fashion as in the progressive inauguration of various facets of one's personality which are to be pursued and developed during the remainder of one's life course.

According to Vaillant, the motive for this development comes from within the individual, though external factors impede or facilitate the movement. From the Grant Study he observes that personal resources as well as external sources of support and guidance were necessary for the developmental gains that these men were able to realize.[8] Vaillant relates the personal resources of individuals to their choice of adaptive mechanisms, the defensive styles which people adopt in response to stress. He describes a gradual maturing in the ways in which people defend against anxiety. This represents a maturing of the ego, the orderly and ordering aspect of the human psyche, which directs a person's adaptive and executive functions. The ego defends against anxiety and danger by employing various mechanisms. These "defense mechanisms" are "unconscious, and *sometimes* pathological, mental processes that the ego uses to resolve conflict among the four lodestars of our inner life: instincts, the real world, important people, and the internalized prohibitions provided by our conscience and our culture."[9]

Vaillant presents a hierarchy of the ego's defensive mechanisms, and he suggests that more mature defenses can and do emerge over the span of adult development. At the lowest level are the "psychotic" mechanisms of delusional projection, denial, and distortion. These are superseded by the immature mechanisms of projection, schizoid fantasy (retreat to fantasy for resolution of a conflict), hypochondriasis, passive-aggressive behavior, and acting out. Both of these groups of defense mechanisms are common in healthy individuals in early life but are normally given up for more mature mechanisms as psychological development continues. A third level of defense mechanisms are those classed as neurotic—intellectualization, repression, displacement, reaction formation, and dissociation. The fourth level consists of the mature mechanisms of altruism, humor, suppression, anticipation, and sublimation.[10]

One of Vaillant's major conclusions is that adult life is a time of growth and that one aspect of this growth is maturation in one's way of adapting to life's circumstances.[11] While Vaillant has a broader focus than just the issues of midlife, he has emphasized the significance of the research for an understanding of midlife turbulence. "Perhaps the most important conclusion of the Grant Study has been that the agonizing self-reappraisal and instinctual reawakening at age 40—the so-called midlife crisis—does not appear to portend decay. However marred by depression and turmoil middle life may be, it often heralds a new stage of man."[12]

Another prominent theorist of adult life, Daniel Levinson, presents the results of his research in *The Seasons of a Man's Life*, research on the lives of forty men drawn from four professions.[13] Like Vaillant, Levinson makes generous use of Erikson's stage theory; but, unlike Vaillant, he pays more attention to social context than to intrapsychic phenomena. Levinson proposes the concept of a life structure based on one's relationships to self and to the external world. By focusing on the changes which life structure (a pattern of relationships to significant others, to institutions, to nature, to objects and places, and to the self) undergoes over the course of life, Levinson is able to arrive at a more comprehensive picture of adult development. During the life course there are periods when one's life structure is either being built up or being changed. The periods of change or transition are times when an individual is terminating one phase of life, striving to become individuated, and initiating a new phase with either a new, or at least a reevaluated, life structure. Levinson assigns approximate

31

chronological ages for each developmental period. Though the ages will vary somewhat among individuals, he says that the sequence is invariable. Each structure building period lasts for about six or seven years and is followed by a structure changing period. For the middle adult era of life, the midlife transition begins at about age forty and ends at about forty-five.[14]

Prior to the midlife transition, Levinson places a period he calls "Becoming One's Own Man," which correlates with Vaillant's stage of career consolidation. This is the time when a man is climbing the ladder of achievement in his occupational role, and it occurs, according to Levinson, in the thirty-six to forty age span. The midlife transition comes around the age of forty; it is a time of great struggle with the self and with the external world. This is a period when one reappraises life in the awareness that one does not stay young forever. Various polarities within the personality are acknowledged and allowed to express themselves. So a man struggles with the young and the old within himself, the masculine and the feminine, his destructive side and his creative side, his desire to be attached to someone or something and yet to be independent. All this leads to certain attempts at modification of the life structure. Levinson maintains that even when life looks externally the same, changes have occurred. With the conclusion of the midlife transition, a person settles down into middle adulthood. The cycles of transition and then stabilization continue throughout the remainder of a person's life.[15]

Psychological research on midlife and the midlife transition is still in its early stages. Consequently we must keep the door open to further theoretical developments and additional research data. Levinson and a number of other theorists draw attention to the fact that early studies did not include the midlife transitions of women. Carol Gilligan has noted the limitations that are inherent when one measures a woman's development against male standards. Her research results, presented in her book *In a Different Voice*, indicate another way of understanding human development which gives more attention to attachment and relationships; this is in contrast to studies based on male subjects which emphasize separation as the hallmark of maturity.[16] Gilligan observes: "In view of the evidence that women perceive and construe social reality differently from men and that these differences center around experiences of attachment and separation, life transitions that invariably engage these experiences can be expected to involve women in a distinctive way. And because women's sense of integrity appears to be entwined with an ethic of care, so that to see themselves as women is to see themselves in a relationship of connection, the major transitions in women's lives would seem to involve changes in the understanding and activities of care."[17]

There are certain pitfalls to be avoided when one is applying the current theories of adult development. Levinson cautions against seeing the stages he has described as a hierarchy in which one stage is better than another.[18] Vaillant notes that general predictions for good adaptive progress cannot be made only on the basis of the individuals which his group studied. "The men's lives are full of surprises, and the Grant Study provides no prediction tables. Rather, the study of lifetimes is comparable to the study of celestial navigation. Neither a sextant nor a celestial map can predict where we *should* go; but both are invaluable in letting us identify where we are."[19]

Bernice Neugarten, a long time researcher of adult development, has recently expressed some reservations about assigning chronological ages to periods in adult development. As she looks at contemporary society, she believes that people's lives are becoming more fluid and varied, age norms and age are becoming less limiting and relevant, and significant life events and role transitions are becoming more irregular.[20] What continues to be important, however, according to Neugarten, is a person's own assessment of being on time in his or her development. "It is not the fact that one reaches 40, 50 or 60 which is itself important, but rather, 'How am I doing for my age?' "[21] In contrast to those who hold that major life events are often the cause of crises, Neugarten maintains that a crisis occurs primarily when a major life event is not on time according to the timetable of a given individual. The death of a loved one is the occasion of crisis when it occurs at an unexpected time, such as at an early age. If the event is on time, it has normally been anticipated and rehearsed and therefore the threat of personal crisis is considerably reduced.[22]

The first use of the term *midlife crisis* is usually attributed to Elliot Jaques.[23] In his study of creative genius, Jaques became aware that a critical stage of development occurs around age thirty-five as illustrated in Richard Church's autobiographical work *The Voyage Home*: "There seems to be a biological reason for men and women, when they reach the middle thirties, finding themselves beset with misgivings, agonizing inquiries, and a loss of zest. Is it that state which the medieval schoolmen called *accidie*, the cardinal sin of spiritual sloth? I believe it is."[24] As a crisis, Jaques concludes this experience may lead in one of three directions. It may lead to the drying up of the creative process in an individual; it may signal the first emergence of creativity; or it may usher in a different type of creativity in which the creative work is changed in quality and content. Jaques presents a coterie of creative people whose lives give evidence of this change of creativity.

Some theorists take issue with Jaques's use of the word *crisis*, and they suggest that *transition* may be a more appropriate designation for the midlife phenomenon which he and others describe. Jaques himself nuances his use of the term *crisis*; it is a period of rapid transition or a phase that is a change point in a person's life. He comments, "The reactions range all the way from severe and dramatic crisis, to a smoother and less troubled transition—just as reactions to the phase of adolescent crisis may range from severe disturbance and breakdown to relatively ordered readjustments to mental and sexual adulthood—but the effects of the change are there to be discerned."[25]

Whatever disagreements there may be with some aspects of Jaques's work, his paper "Death and the Mid-Life Crisis" remains a classic in the interpretation and analysis of midlife processes and creativity. Although his study originally focused on the effects that the passage through midlife had on the creativity of three hundred recognized artistic figures, he has substantiated its broader applicability. Jaques drew attention to what he called "sculpted creativity," a changed mode of producing creative work from a person's late thirties on. What may have come through sudden inspiration or what may have been zealously executed in the early lives of many creative people emerges only slowly and with considerable effort at midlife. At times the inspiration may be quick, but the process of working and reworking the inspiration is drawn out, as if a person were sculpting in stone. Jaques also points to a change in the quality of the creative work which accompanies the "sculpting" of midlife creativity. A tragic or a philosophical component in the creative work at this period of life leads to a new serenity, which is achievable because one has learned to accept struggle and pain in life.[26] The way people achieve this more mature form of creativity is the subject of Jaques's study.

Depression, Turbulence, and the Midlife Transition

Most researchers recognize that there is a period of depression and some turbulence connected with the midlife passage. Vaillant speaks of a "second adolescence," a period marked by instinctual reawakening and a reassessing or reordering of the past especially of one's relationship to one's parents; for midlife is another period of psychological weaning. The depression is occasioned by having to accept pain and destructiveness in life and in oneself. It is a time when one mourns the loss of a view of life which fit the youthful ambitions of the early thirties but is no longer adequate.[27] But, as Vaillant notes, "such transitional periods in life provide a means of seizing one more chance and finding a new solution to old instinctual or interpersonal needs."[28] Levinson, relying heavily on Jaques, reports that a man may even appear "sick" or "upset" to those around him as he goes through these struggles and turmoil. In women's development, Gilligan observes: "The events of mid-life—the menopause and changes in family and work—can alter a woman's activities of care in ways that affect her sense of herself. If mid-life brings an end to relationships, to the sense of connection on which she relies, as well as to the activities of care through which she judges her worth, then the mourning that accompanies all life transitions can give way to the melancholia of self-depreciation and despair."[29]

People are sometimes horrified by what they see in themselves at midlife. In the process of examining one's life, unconscious conflicts are activated. Unresolved emotional issues of earlier life stages can hold a person back from making important changes in his or her life structure. "Every genuine reappraisal must be agonizing, because it challenges the illusions and vested interests on which the existing structure is based."[30]

According to psychiatrist Judd Marmor the recurring stress during this time takes the form of separation loss.[31] Consciously a person loses his or her youthful self-image; and friends and relatives die. On an unconscious level, the more unrealistic hopes for security, fame, and achievement which were operative in the first half of life also die as a person makes compromises with reality. Even more painful is the acceptance of the gradual physical deterioration which is an inevitable consequence of the aging process. As a person confronts their own death, they surrender the fantasy of earthly immortality. This confrontation with mortality brings a person face to face with existential anxiety, a terror and fear that well up when one is faced with the limits of human existence. Yet it is in this largely unconscious struggle with anxiety that one can discover a renewed vitality for creative engagement with life. In one sense the struggle is not entirely new, for the present phase in human experience is always connected with the dynamic, albeit unconscious, memories of the past. The terror which is experienced in the depths of the human psyche at midlife is a primitive feeling which has its roots in the very first period of human life. Its reemergence enables a person to deal with it with increased rational powers and to resolve the early infantile conflict more adequately. This continuity which is found throughout all the stages of human life has been poetically described by Proust in his *Remembrance of Things Past*: "For man is that creature without any fixed age, who has the faculty of becoming, in a few seconds, many years younger, and who, surrounded by the walls of time through which he has lived, floats within them but as though in a basin, the surface level of which is constantly changing, so as to bring him into the range now of one epoch, now of another."[32]

The most insightful commentator on the reworking of the infantile conflict during midlife is Elliott Jaques. To explain the change in the creative process at midlife, Jaques points to a change in the very mind of the artist. The creator has left behind the idealism and optimism of late adolescence and early adulthood and has come to accept a less perfect vision of the world and of the self. The creative person still holds to the overriding goodness of people and the self, but there is a recognition and acceptance of hate and destructiveness present along with that goodness. Formerly this hate and destructiveness contributed to the artist's misery and unhappiness. Midlife resignation to the inevitability of death and to the presence of hate and destructive impulses within oneself signals the achievement of mature adulthood.[33]

To clarify further, Jaques describes mature adulthood as a reworking of what is called the "depressive position," a stage in infant psychological development which is described in the works of Melanie Klein, a pioneer in an object relations theory of personality.[34] The advent of this stage occurs with a child's efforts to relate to the mother as a person who both satisfies and frustrates him or her. As the frustrator of the infant's desires for total satisfaction, the mother is the object of the child's aggressive and destructive feelings. She is seen as related only to the child, who, caring nothing for her independent existence, would like to take her, the food provider, inside itself. Somewhere along the line of infant development, the child senses that the "good mother" (the provider) and the "bad mother" (the frustrator) are one and the same person. The child begins to sense that mother is a whole object in which it finds both good and bad. It senses, too, that the very one on whom its well-being depends is the same one whom it has wished to destroy and take into itself. But now the child begins to feel concern for the mother and goes through a period of depressive anxiety related to the feeling of almost having lost or destroyed the mother on whom it depends. This depressive anxiety is dealt with through reparation and the channeling of strong feelings in other directions than toward the mother; in short, this is the beginning of sublimation. This first experience of ambivalent feeling, now seen as directed to the same object, is critically important for later development. The depressive position is reactivated in later stages of life when the individual is afforded opportunities, such as in periods of mourning, to work it through more fully and with more mature insight.

Because the memories of these early experiences are buried deep in the unconscious, a person at midlife may have no idea of the depth of the work going on within themselves. He or she only notices the emotional exhaustion and exasperation, which seem out of proportion to their conscious assessment of the current situation. What does come to mind, though, is that with the passing of youth there is now something to be mourned and one's own eventual death is to be anticipated. This forces a person to come to terms with personal destructiveness and hate. The desire to totally control one's environment and one's future, frequently through a close relationship with God, the all-good provider, has proven to be unrealizable. Plagued by unfulfilled dreams and by shattered ideals, persons at midlife find that the enemy of their fulfillment and happiness is less outside themselves in other people or in situations and more within, in their own hearts. They experience their internal chaos in terms of not knowing what they want, what they care for, or if anything is worthwhile. Rather than being fulfilled, they feel drained by all they have done in their lives. Life looks like a series of losses with the greatest loss, that of life itself, still ahead.

Judd Marmor describes four patterns of reaction to these inner anxieties which are experienced at midlife. The first of these reactions is to deny one's inner confusion by escape. This may take various forms. Total immersion in a hectic social life can keep a person so busy that he or she does not have time to face the self. Excessive consumption of alcohol or other drugs and sexual promiscuity can deaden the sensitivities of the human spirit so that the real issues are never adequately dealt with. Ever-increasing work involvements can lead to the abandonment of any serious self-reflection. And thus evasion becomes the dominant reaction pattern of life.

Secondly, there can be denial by overcompensation. Here work enters the picture. The prodigious amount of work that persons may force themselves to do can effectively block out feelings of growing old and having to slow down. An attempt to recapture the feelings of youth reveals itself in increasing attention devoted to bodily appearance so as to eliminate any trace of aging. Interest in music, sports, and possessions may even follow the lines advocated by the youth culture. Many previous interests are surrendered.

A third reaction pattern to the stresses of midlife is decompensation. When the stress is so great that persons feel unable to cope with it by ordinary means, they may move to lower levels of psychological functioning, for example, severe depression, unaccustomed anxiety, apathetic surrender, or intense feelings of rage. All these represent attempts to come to terms with the threatening situation of midlife.[36]

The fourth of Marmor's patterns of reaction is a movement to a higher level of integration through emotional acceptance of loss and change. Jaques speaks of this achievement as a successful working through of the depressive position. Here hate, which is experienced in memory, is mitigated by love; death and destructiveness are answered by the will to live, to build up, and to repair; damage caused by destructiveness is healed by loving grief and a sense of regained vitality. A renewed sense of confidence and hope comes about because the self is experienced as capable of enduring loss and grief and of overcoming the feelings of guilt and persecution which are connected with the hurt one's own destructiveness has caused. Envy of others' youth and of their accomplishments can be replaced by a sense of admiration for them and a sense of gratitude for one's own life with its unique richness.[37]

In this reaction pattern, to use Erikson's terminology, there is a

38

movement toward that virtue of the last stage of life, namely, wisdom. "It is the acceptance of one's own and only life cycle and of the people who have become significant to it as something that had to be and that, by necessity, permitted of no substitutions. It thus means a new and different love of one's parents, free of the wish that they should have been different, and an acceptance of the fact that one's life is one's own responsibility. It is a sense of comradeship with men and women of distant times and of different pursuits, who have created orders and objects and sayings conveying human dignity and love."[38] This movement out of depressive anxiety would also represent for Erikson a cultivation of an attitude of care. This attitude is summed up in what Erikson sees as the ethical rule of adulthood—"to do to others what will help them, even as it helps you, to grow."[39]

While Jaques emphasizes the good results of a midlife passage out of depressive anxiety when love dominates hate and destructiveness, he does not mean to suggest that the passage is easy. He speaks of it as "essentially a period of purgatory." Through it all, a person grows in the capacity to accept and tolerate conflict and ambivalence. Such a capacity has a direct bearing on how a person goes about his or her creative work. "One's work need no longer be experienced as perfect. It can be worked and reworked, but it will be accepted as having shortcomings."[40] A person learns to accept work which is "good enough" in the realization that there will always be inevitable imperfection. Rather than having imperfection create a sense of failure, it is accepted with a resignation which imparts to the work a sense of serenity.

Furthermore, there is a sense of detachment with respect to the creative inspiration, so that it is released into the external world, is influenced by that world, and returns to enrich the worker. No longer is there a sense of being drained and left empty by one's creative efforts. The completed object of a person's creative effort becomes a part of their internal world and colors and enriches their self-understanding. Creative workers do not die because of their external efforts; their lives become fuller. Death itself can be faced with more equanimity, because the fear of death is perceived as a temporal prelude to the experience of new life. A sense of wholeness emerges based on the sufficient goodness of the self and the objects—persons, places, and things—which make up the internal world of people's minds, the living memories on which they all depend.

People, in effect, become artists of their own lives, as they work and rework the various strands of their life tapestry. Some of these strands are from very early life, those which centered around interactions with parents. Vaillant maintains that full maturity in adulthood can only be achieved when one's parents are discovered to be internalized, living on inside one's mind. There, living within the person, the parents can provide fresh strength. In psychological language, Vaillant sums up the matter this way: "to internalize and to identify is to grow." He goes on to address the apparent strangeness of this formulation. "How can a person, unless literally pregnant, take another person inside? Certainly psychoanalysts speak of individuals *incorporating, introjecting,* and *internalizing* other people; but is not that just a part of the myth-making process of the Freudian imagination? A moment's reflection upon religious sacraments (e.g. taking in the blood and body of Christ through communion wine and wafer) or education (e.g. absorbing the professor's wisdom) or falling in love (e.g. she lives on inside my heart) suggest that taking the *corpora* of another person *in* is a metaphor not confined to psychoanalysis."[41]

The processes of internalization and identification continue throughout life. Both the good and the bad aspects of parents have been taken in. During the life course the individual may work unconsciously to strengthen or weaken some of these identifications. One of the tasks of a midlife transition is in some way to come to terms with these identifications. The degree of success a religious person has in this process will have repercussions on his or her image of God, which is built upon the early childhood experiences of one's parents. This will be explored more fully in a later chapter.

The timetable of the midlife passage, while it is a great concern, cannot be precisely fixed; for the tasks of any developmental period often go on beyond conscious awareness. To this extent they are not items that can be entered into an appointment calendar or a long-range plan. Nevertheless, an awareness of what is going on within oneself can foster an appreciation of the approximate length of time (usually several years) required to make the midlife transition.

Developmental Tasks in the Midlife Transition

Here and throughout this study the focus is on the period of adult life which roughly spans the two decades from age thirty-five to age fifty-five. This period begins with some recognition that life has reached a midpoint and that consequently some adjustments have to be made. These adjustments or adaptations are designated here as the ten tasks of midlife transition.[42]

1 Shifting the Time Perspective

At midlife time becomes a preoccupation or concern. There is a growing awareness that one's yesterdays outnumber the tomorrows of life. Time is perceived to be running out, for life itself and especially for accomplishing all that had been hoped for and planned. This shift in outlook is brought about by the inevitable bodily changes that occur as one gets older, as well as by the experience of role reversals. People are no longer recipients of care and supervision, but they now experience themselves as caregivers and supervisors of the young. Persons at midlife see how their own parents have aged and need care. With all this comes a renewed preoccupation with their past childhood and adolescence and a sense of concern about their own old age. Their whole life cycle comes into view in a way in which it has never appeared before. In American society, which puts so much emphasis on youth and vigor, people at midlife often have a sense of uneasiness as they move into the generation in the middle. Whereas in the past people felt that they were changing faster than those around them, now they feel that the world and people around them are changing faster than they are.[43] A sense of urgency can sweep over a person. In the dramatic phrase of Gail Sheehy, age thirty-five to forty-five is the "deadline decade."[44]

2 Assessing the Limits of Achievement

With the shift in time perspective there also comes a review of the personal timetable. "Can I realistically accomplish what I had hoped I would?" "Maybe I have to settle for a lesser degree of success?" Midlife presents an opportunity for assessing more carefully the extent of one's abilities and talents and coming to some acceptance of the limits which they imply. Acceptance means either an adjustment of expectations or a stronger push to use more of those abilities. Either way, a person has to realize that others may accomplish more than he or she will, no matter how hard one tries.[45]

For the creative person midlife can be a harrowing time. Trying to assess what can realistically be done, choosing some things for execution and rejecting others, all this can be excruciatingly difficult. "This reality-testing is the more severe the greater is the creative ability of the individual, for the time scale of creative work increases dramatically with ability. Thus the experience is particularly painful in genius, capable of achieving vastly more than it is possible to achieve in the remaining years, and therefore frustrated by the immense vision of things to be done which will not be done."[46]

3   Dealing with One's Envy and Rivalry

In order to enjoy and be grateful for the accomplishments of others, people must deal with their own rivalrous and envious feelings. This is possible through an acceptance and appreciation of what they themselves are able to do despite their shortcomings and imperfections. A successful negotiation of the midlife transition requires a willingness to see oneself as part of a larger whole and, thus, as having a concern for others within that larger context. A desperate clinging to power and an attempt to control all aspects of one's work reveals an inability to see one's contributions as part of a shared generational goal. Furthermore, if one constantly fears one's position will be taken by the young or strives to unseat those in superior positions, this is to fail at self-acceptance and to attempt to live mature adulthood according to the patterns of early childhood conflicts. Part of midlife maturation involves coming to terms with the personal myths of envy or rivalry which underlie a series of repeated relationships throughout the first part of life.[47] The search for adulation and acclaim from a coterie of admirers no longer appears to be worthwhile in the light of one's proven talents and abilities.

4   Balancing Polarities

Another task for persons in midlife is the integration of opposing tendencies within themselves. Levinson speaks of these opposing tendencies as polarities and cites four pairs which are the focus of midlife efforts at individuation: young/old, destruction/creation, masculine/feminine, and attachment/separation.[48] The task at midlife is to acknowledge both sides of each pair in one's life. Persons at midlife must allow room in their expression and understanding of themselves for both the masculine and the feminine elements. While striving to be creative persons, they must accept and attempt to counteract the destructiveness which they find in themselves and in their dealings with others. Separateness from other people and from things is balanced out by the equally important need for attachment. At midlife, when persons begin to realize their advancing age, they also begin to realize that in many ways they are young. Working with the polarities of human existence is a life-long task. While integration of these polarities may advance at midlife, it is not achieved in any final fashion.

5 Standing Up to an Aggressive World

The ordinary human environment always contains its share of frustrating and irritating people and circumstances. Envy, narrow-mindedness, corruption, and sadism are found in one form or another in every organization and institution where people engage in ordinary human commerce. Everyone can expect to receive attacks which spring from the ignoble aspects of other people and organizations.[49] Marjorie Fiske, a researcher and theorist of adult development, sees the conflict between individual commitments and organizational methods and goals as the cause of some midlife crises.[50] Persons who consider themselves altruistic may find that the organizations to which they belong not only operate differently but also are opposed to personal value-orientations in significant areas.

To face the attacks of an aggressive world realistically is an important task at midlife. This means standing up to them without denial, undue submission, and unreflective rebelliousness. In order to counter the tendency to exploit the weaknesses of the system or to be corrupted by it, fidelity to one's ideals has to be tested and strengthened in the unavoidable conflicts of the real world. What matters is the ability to accept final responsibility for oneself.

6 Reevaluating the Life Structure

Another task for the person in midlife is to examine and to try to make sense of the various parts of his or her life. All relationships—to self, to people, places, organizations, and things—can be called into question and be the subject of examination. In Levinson's terminology, these relationships make up the fabric of one's life structure. At a

43

time of transition persons realize that they have choices; they can choose to modify some of these relationships and so change their life structure, or they can recommit themselves to their existing life structure. In any case, the task here is the willingness to enter into this process of reevaluation.[51]

Marjorie Fiske has written about the process of reordering commitments. Her research and that of her associates have shown that "the sense of well-being was far more likely to be associated with the sense of past and future changes in goals and behavior patterns than with continuity."[52] If such changes are not to be overly disruptive of a stable sense of self, a self which endures despite change, Fiske sees the need for moratoria, times for getting hold of the sense of the self as continuous. "The committed, as they undergo inner and outer change, find new meanings in their lives when they allow themselves the moratoria required for coping with successive life stages within a rapidly changing socio-historical context."[53] In the process of reordering commitments, Fiske maintains that the first commitment is to self-discovery and rediscovery.

7 Facing Loss, Mourning, and Death

For a person to undergo personal change is to leave behind a former state of affairs; it is to lose a former way of relating to the self or to the external world. Some changes are brought about by a person's own choices; some are outside a person's control, such as the change which results from economic or professional misfortune. The challenge is to face the loss which is part of the life experience without excessive anxiety and with sufficient belief in oneself and one's personal resources to weather the storm. The loss involved in change requires that there be mourning of what is passing or past and what will be no more. This mourning process is kept within appropriate bounds when people are aware that they have striven to do their best toward themselves and toward those with whom they have been involved. Such awareness enables people to begin to mourn their own deaths, knowing that they have fulfilled their missions in life to the best of their ability. The mourning process is also softened by the realization that one continues living on in people whom one has loved and in the tangible results of creative work.[54]

Accepting the death of parents is a significant part of midlife

44

mourning for some people. In *Mourning and Melancholia* Freud drew attention to identification with a lost object as a means to the resolution of the mourning process.[55] To identify is to assimilate aspects of the other person and to be transformed according to the model which the other provides. This means not only taking into oneself the qualities of the parents but also the relationships to them which comprise the world a person has shared with them. A person becomes internally enriched by the world of the parents and strives to keep it alive within the self.[56]

8 Cultivating Care

In his study "Normal Narcissism in Middle Age," psychoanalyst Otto Kernberg has observed: "The repeated work of recreating and consolidating the world of one's parents also increases the tolerance for the ambivalence of and toward one's children, and the freedom for maintaining, increasing, and deepening the interest in their own independently growing world."[57] In a broader spectrum of relationships than simply that of parents to children, the internal possession of the world of one's own parents provides a sense of security which allows interactions with the young without intense envy or aggressive competitiveness. An awareness of one's own internal richness allows a person to develop a care and concern for those who are coming after.

Erikson associates the virtue of care with the mature side of adulthood. By virtue he understands a vital strength which is necessary for an individual's life cycle and the cycle of generations within society, where generativity in its widest sense can relate to the mature drive to generate and regenerate products and ideas. Care emerges as the successful resolution of what Erikson calls the crisis of generativity versus stagnation or self-absorption. "In that mature state [of adulthood], fate, as well as the life lived so far, decides whom and what one is committed to take care of so as to assure the next generation's life and strength."[58] Regarding women's development, Gilligan says: "Since the reality of connection is experienced by women as given rather than as freely contracted, they arrive at an understanding of life that reflects the limits of autonomy and control. As a result, women's development delineates the path not only to a less violent life but also to a maturity realized through interdependence and taking care."[59]

45

9 Gaining Wisdom

The last psychosocial stage in the life cycle according to Erikson is integrity versus despair and disgust. The virtue central to this stage is wisdom. Erikson's description of wisdom draws attention to the strength gained through a struggle with despair and disgust. "Wisdom . . . is the detached and yet active concern with life itself in the face of death itself, and . . . it maintains and conveys the integrity of experience in spite of Disdain over human failing and the Dread of ultimate non-being."[60] To live in despair is to live with the feeling that life is too short to try another route that would lead to a sense of wholeness. The cloak for such despair is often a contemptuous attitude toward certain people and institutions, a distrust of others, and a display of disgust for life. All these external attitudes are really displacements of the disdain for oneself. A person who can counter despair lives within the wisdom which comes with the achievement of integrity.

10 Searching for the Other

In "Reflections on Dr. Borg's Life Cycle" Erikson uses Ingmar Bergman's movie *Wild Strawberries* to present a conception of the life cycle and the generational cycle. The central figure in the movie is a seventy-six year old doctor. On the day the movie takes place, he is to receive a doctorate for fifty years of service in his profession. The movie depicts the day-long journey of the doctor and his thirty-eight year old daughter-in-law from his home to the city of Lund. At midday the pair, now joined by some young hitchhikers, stop for gas and for lunch. In the midst of their noon meal the doctor is prompted to recite a poem. After beginning the recitation, he stumbles for some lines, and his daughter-in-law comes to his assistance. The two actually alternate the lines of the short poem.

> Where is the friend I seek everywhere?
> Dawn is the time of loneliness and care . . .
> When twilight comes, I am still yearning.
> I see His trace of glory and power,
> In an ear of grain and the fragrance of a flower,
> In every sign and breath of air,
> His love is there.

Commenting on the poem, its context and tone, Erikson observes that there is a religious dimension to every person's integrity.[61] This dimension is found in the inner search for the Other, in the wish to communicate with the mysterious Other. The reason for this, Erikson notes, has to do with the fact that there can be no "I" without an "Other." In the doctor's old age, he longs to recapture life's early moments of complete affirmation and love. Life is cyclic for Erikson because it rounds itself out. Bergman's peopling this luncheon scene with the midlife daughter-in-law and the youthful hitchhikers seems to attest to the place of this religious dimension throughout the life cycle.

That there is a perpetual longing in the human heart, which no amount of human effort can remove or satisfy, is more than a theological statement on the human condition. It also finds its place in psychological reflections on the relative nature of human fulfillment or integration. In one of her final works, "On the Sense of Loneliness," Melanie Klein remarks: "In conclusion I wish to restate my hypothesis that although loneliness can be diminished or increased by external influences, it can never be completely eliminated, because the urge towards integration, as well as the pain experienced in the process of integration, spring from internal sources which remain powerful throughout life."[62]

While these ten developmental tasks provide a helpful way to think about the psychic work that everyone needs to do at midlife, an overview of the whole transformation process at this stage is also important for spiritual directors. Furthermore, the role which another person can play in facilitating an individual's growth needs to be highlighted. Roger Gould, George Vaillant, and Daniel Levinson have all drawn attention to the important contribution which a friend or mentor can make to another person's development. These theorists suggest the importance of a spiritual director's contribution to a person at midlife.

Transformations

In his book *Transformations*, a presentation of growth and change in adult life, Roger Gould speaks about the movement throughout adult life away from a "childhood consciousness."[63] In a more technical essay, Gould defines transformation as an expansion of self-definition.[64] He points out how the boundaries of the self-definition can be extremely limited. As soon as a person steps across these boundaries in some risk-taking behavior, anxiety appears as well as a sense of internal prohibition. To undergo a transformation is to expand the boundaries of a self-definition thereby overcoming stagnation and suffocation and achieving a sense of vitality and increased inner freedom. The way a person reaches such a transformation is by uncovering false ideas about reality and the self which hold him or her back. Attempts at this uncovering lead to an experience of warfare within the person; this is often externalized onto some other relationship or situation, for it is often easier for a person to acknowledge enemies without than within.[65] However, important agents or catalysts in the transformational process are found outside in a person's relationships with others. These persons Gould calls friends to growth. They are "those who respond openly to what we are becoming, those who endorse and confirm our expanded selves." Sometimes such people are found outside the ordinary work place or network of relationships. The desire to confirm and vitalize underdeveloped parts of the self leads a person to seek out such helpers to growth. For, as Gould succinctly puts it, "all parts human are originally born in mutuality."[66]

Gould is not the only researcher and theorist who draws attention to the importance of other people for assisting the growth process of adult life. Vaillant suggests that the acquisition of more mature adaptive styles is facilitated by apprenticeship. "Both as children and adults, we learn to anticipate future pain effectively only if someone first sits beside us while we learn to bear current anxiety."[67] While Vaillant does not hold that adaptive styles can be taught, he does believe that they can be absorbed. In the lives of the Grant study subjects, Vaillant discovered that these men "did require, at crucial, if unidentified, times during their lives, close relationships with benign individuals, who could serve as models and as positive objects for identification."[68]

Levinson singles out a mentor relationship as of special importance in the adult development of the subjects whom he studied. Normally a mentor is prominent in early adult life, helping a young person to enter into the adult world. When persons are in their late thirties, they are helped by mentors to move toward individuation, the process of becoming more their own persons. The midlife transition is the time during which people realize that they themselves will soon assume mentor roles with respect to younger people. Developmentally, mentor relationships are significant because they provide situations in which the recipients can identify with someone who embodies qualities which they themselves desire.[69] Following some formulations of the psychoanalyst D. W. Winnicott, Levinson sees the mentor as a transitional figure who, when he is "good enough," is "an admixture of a good father and a good friend."[70]

A person's relationship with a mentor can itself be the scene of struggle and hardship because it can call forth old patterns of relating to parents and reawaken childhood expectations and disappointments. Levinson, describing the male perspective, sees this in terms of a man struggling with the little boy still present within himself: "The little boy desperately wants the mentor to be a good father in the most childish sense—a father who will make him special, will endow him with magical powers and will not require him to compete or prove himself in relation to would-be rivals. It is also the little boy who anxiously makes the mentor into a bad father—a depriving, dictatorial authority who has no real love and merely uses one for his own needs. The relationship is made untenable by the yearning for the good father, the anxiety over the bad father, and the projection of both of these internal figures onto the mentor, who is then caught in the bind."[71] However, this difficulty can be worked through with the assistance of a mentor who is attuned to what is happening. Thus, to be a good mentor Levinson holds that a person must have successfully done the work of his or her own midlife transition.

It should be evident that Levinson's comments about the mentor relationship have direct relevance to this study of spiritual direction for people in midlife transition. Indeed, the psychological research on midlife and midlife transitions underscores in its own way the centrality of the quest for truth throughout life, the same quest which animates the process of spiritual direction. The truth in both instances has to do with the self and its relationships to both internal and external reality. This is a truth arrived at by stripping off childish overlays and the protective coverings of immaturity. To allow the truth to emerge is to undergo a transformation. The process of transformation brings more and more freedom as a person moves closer to the truth, but the transformational process is never finished.

Spiritual Direction and Perspectives on Midlife

Like Levinson's mentor, the spiritual directors of people in mid-life transition try to be sensitive to the various issues which are before the persons whom they are directing. Adult life is complex and dynamic both psychologically and spiritually. A growing body of both psychological and theological literature on adult development gives evidence of the ongoing nature of reflection and research in both areas. With this wealth of material available, it is possible to acquire a great deal of information about the various challenges and problems of adult spiritual and psychological development. Practitioners, however, may feel more weighed down by all this information than freed for more skilled directing. Their purpose, after all, is not to give lectures *about* direction but to exercise a refined listening and to make sensitive responses using the well-recognized vocabulary of faith. Their questions are practical—how can they best use the theological knowledge they have already acquired and incorporate into it continuing theological reflection and the best of an ever-growing body of psychological research and theory? How can they best do this for the benefit of Christians in midlife transition? How can they more adequately grasp the human situations of these people?

People and human situations are multifaceted. They can be looked at in one way and then in another. The viewpoints are really complementary, and by putting some of these viewpoints together a person can achieve a fuller understanding of the reality being looked at.[72] In this study we have looked at the midlife transition from the viewpoints of spirituality and psychology. We considered the phenomenon of midlife change from both perspectives. Each of these perspectives has illuminated different aspects of the transition. At times both have pointed to the same experiences of the midlife transition but have labeled them with names drawn from their respective vocabularies. These names are not just superimposed on reality in order to better theorize about it. Rather, they are terms which are intended to reveal the dynamic state of affairs which people are experiencing; this is meant to facilitate helping and understanding these people. In other words, the names are intended to lead people to think more deeply about the reality of the situation. To designate a midlife situation of turmoil and turbulence as an aspect of *conversion* is to suggest a dynamic pattern which leads to seeing the turmoil

50

differently. Likewise, to call that same situation a *transition* is to suggest a developmental framework for what otherwise might be viewed apart from the whole life course.

The predominant perspective which spiritual directors use in their work is that of spiritual theology. They usually try to read situations in terms of God's actions within people, of grace as a dynamic operative in human life which leads to greater love and service. They see the obstacles to grace as sinful conditions which can become the focus of further efforts at conversion. Religious language, made up of terms such as grace and sin, provides spiritual directors with various handles for grasping the human situation. Their assessment of people and their situations constitutes a diagnosis—a way of knowing and understanding what they face so that together directors and directees may do the right thing. As psychologist Paul Pruyser has expressed it more formally: "Diagnosis in any helping profession is the exploratory process in which the troubled person is given an opportunity to assess and evaluate himself in a defined perspective, in which certain observations are made and specific data come to light, guided by conceptual and operational tools, in a personal relationship with a resource person."[73] The diagnosis which is carried out in the context of spiritual direction is a theological or pastoral one; it is made primarily out of a theological perspective, and it employs religious language.[74]

Keeping these ideas of perspective and diagnosis in mind can give a greater sense of clarity and purpose to the work of spiritual directors. Their direction of people at midlife may be only a segment of the work they do with many other people, but it provides them with an opportunity to refine their use of theological perspectives and it further develops their diagnostic skills. This is so because at midlife, as David Burrell has demonstrated, religious terms take on fresh meanings. Burrell sees the church as a community of discourse where a particular language receives a hallowed usage and where stories of faith are told and reenacted. "In coming to know the church as we have, we can recognize how she offers an ensemble of symbolic expressions and performances which exercise us in addressing what it is to be and to become a human being. We learn how to use the expressions as we participate in the activities; and to allow the expressions to guide us in finding our way is to let them shape our lives."[75] By furnishing a religious language, the church creates a context within which a person can become an individual. In the chapters which follow, we will give attention to a number of key terms in the language of the church which can illuminate the struggles and progress of people at midlife.

While the theological perspective should be the principal one used by spiritual directors, we suggest that their work with people at midlife will be enhanced by their also using the perspectives of developmental psychology. Some of these perspectives, particularly those which spring from Freudian psychoanalytic theory, might at first seem antithetical to the Gospel spirit and the values which should always animate spiritual direction. For instance, the psychoanalytic image of human beings has been interpreted as contradictory to the theological image because of psychoanalysis's emphasis on unconscious forces, determinism, causality, reductionism, and instinctual motivation. To be sure, there is a dialectical tension between these two images. The Jesuit psychoanalyst W. W. Meissner has discussed these contrasting images and shown, however, that recent development within psychoanalytic thinking has found these two images approximating each other.[76] The rapprochement which he describes indicates that there is fruitful dialogue going on in a number of areas. Psychology no longer is seen as vitiating faith; rather, it can render faith more pure from a human standpoint and contribute to its strengthening.

In this study we are assuming that spiritual direction should be professional work of high calibre, requiring careful thinking, a refined listening ability, and a capacity for empathy with people in the uniqueness of their life situations. A Christian at midlife who seeks spiritual direction presents a particular challenge to the ability and sensitivity of the one who directs. And yet spiritual direction always remains direction in and by the Spirit. A director works to the best of his or her ability in the humble awareness that the Spirit is present and operative. The director strives to enable a person to hear and respond to the Spirit more fully. The director's principal concern is that the Holy Spirit be recognized and distinguished from the many other spirits which can influence people's lives. A midlife transition provides an opportunity for a person to move closer to the truth about himself or herself. Truth is the domain of the Spirit, and it is there that freedom is found.

Notes to Chapter Two

1. Jung, pp. 71, 100, 106–10.

2. Erik H. Erikson, *Childhood and Society*, 2nd ed. (New York: W. W. Norton, 1963), pp. 247–74.

3. Erik H. Erikson, *Identity and the Life Cycle*, Psychological Issues, Vol. I, No. 1 (New York: International Universities Press, 1959), p. 52

4. *Ibid.*, p. 61.

5. (Boston: Little, Brown and Co., 1977).

6. *Ibid.*, pp. 195–236.

7. George Vaillant, "Adaptation to Life," a presentation at "In Celebration of Life Transitions," a conference sponsored by the Continuing Education Department of the University of Kansas and The Center for Applied Behavioral Sciences of The Menninger Foundation, 1980 (audiotape).

8. *Adaptation to Life*, p. 203.

9. *Ibid.*, p. 9.

10. *Ibid.*, pp. 383–86.

11. *Ibid.*, pp. 370–71.

12. George E. Vaillant and Charles A. McArthur, "Natural History of Male Psychologic Health. I. The Adult Life Cycle from 18–50," *Seminars in Psychiatry*, 4 (1972), 427.

13. (New York: Alfred A. Knopf, 1978).

14. *Ibid.*, pp. 40–68.

15. *Ibid.*, pp. 317–40.

16. *In a Different Voice: Psychological Theory and Women's Development* (Cambridge, Mass.: Harvard University Press, 1982).

17. *Ibid.*, p. 171. For a less critical application of Levinson's life-cycle sequence to women's development, see Anita Spencer, *Seasons: Women's Search for Self Through Life's Stages* (New York: Paulist Press, 1982).

18. Daniel J. Levinson, "Toward a Conception of the Adult Life Course," in *Themes of Work and Love in Adulthood*, ed. by Neil J. Smelser and Erik H. Erikson (Cambridge, Mass.: Harvard University Press, 1980), p. 280.

19. Vaillant, *Adaptation to Life*, p. 373.

20. Bernice L. Neugarten, "Time, Age, and the Life Cycle," *American Journal of Psychiatry*, 136 (1979), 888.

21. *Ibid.*; see also Robert C. Peck, "Psychological Developments in the Second Half of Life," in *Middle Age and Aging*, ed. by Bernice L. Neugarten (Chicago: University of Chicago Press, 1968), pp. 88–92.

22. Neugarten, "Time, Age, and the Life Cycle," p. 889.

23. Elliott Jaques, "Death and the Mid-Life Crisis," in *The Interpretation of Death*, ed. by Hendrik M. Ruitenbeek (New York: Jason Aronson, 1973), pp. 140–65, reprinted from *International Journal of Psycho-Analysis*, 46 (1965), 502–14.

24. Cited in Jaques, p. 140.

25. *Ibid.*, p. 143.

26. *Ibid.*, pp. 143–45.

27. Vaillant, *Adaptation to Life*, pp. 219–30.

28. *Ibid.*, p. 222.

29. Gilligan, p. 171.

30. Levinson, *The Season's of a Man's Life*, p. 199.

31. Judd Marmor, "The Crisis of Middle Age," in *Psychiatry in Transition* (New York: Brunner/Mazel, 1974), pp. 71–76.

32. Marcel Proust, *Remembrance of Things Past*, Vol. 2, trans. by C. K. S. Moncrieff (London: Chatto and Windus, 1968), p. 272.

33. Jaques, pp. 146–47.

34. Melanie Klein, *Envy and Gratitude & Other Works: 1946–1963* (New York: Dell, 1977), pp. 71–80; see also Hanna Segal, *Introduction to the Work of Melanie Klein*, 2nd ed. (New York: Basic Books, 1974), pp. 67–81.

35. Marmor, pp. 75–76.

36. See Karl Menninger with Martin Mayman and Paul Pruyser, *The Vital Balance: The Life Process in Mental Health and Illness* (New York: Penguin Books, 1963), esp. pp. 76–124 for an understanding of human behavior from the standpoint of adaptation.

37. Jaques, pp. 161–63.

38. Erikson, *Identity and the Life Cycle*, p. 98.

39. Erik H. Erikson, "Reflections on Dr. Borg's Life Cycle," in *Adulthood*, ed. by Erik H. Erikson (New York: W. W. Norton, 1978), p. 11.

40. Jaques, p. 163.

41. Vaillant, *Adaptation to Life*, p. 344.

42. Although his focus is on a broader period of life than is the concern here, this section is partially dependent on an organizational scheme used in Otto Kernberg's "Normal Narcissism in Middle Age," in *Internal World and External Reality: Object Relations Theory Applied* (New York: Jason Aronson, 1980), pp. 121–34.

43. *Ibid.*, pp. 124–26; Marmor, pp. 72–73; Neugarten, "Time, Age, and the Life Cycle," p. 890.

44. Sheehy, p. 349.

45. Kernberg, pp. 126–27; Jaques, p. 150.

46. Jaques, p. 164.

47. Kernberg, pp. 130–34.

48. Levinson, *The Seasons of a Man's Life*, pp. 209–44.

49. Kernberg, p. 128.

50. Marjorie Fiske, "Changing Hierarchies of Commitment in Adulthood," in *Themes of Work and Love in Adulthood*, ed. by Smelser and Erikson, pp. 246–47.

51. Levinson, *The Seasons of a Man's Life*, pp. 49–56.

52. Fiske, p. 244.

53. *Ibid.*, p. 260.

54. Kernberg, p. 129; Jaques, pp. 161–63.

55. In *Standard Edition of the Complete Psychological Works of Sigmund Freud*, Vol. 14, ed. by James Strachey (London: Hogarth Press, 1955), pp. 243–58.

56. Kernberg, pp. 132–34.

57. *Ibid.*, p. 133.

58. Erikson, "Reflections on Dr. Borg's Life Cycle," p. 7.

59. Gilligan, p. 172.

60. Erikson, "Reflections on Dr. Borg's Life Cycle," p. 26.

61. *Ibid.*, pp. 11–12.

62. Klein, p. 313.

63. *Transformations: Growth and Change in Adult Life* (New York: Simon and Schuster, 1978).

64. "Transformations During Early and Middle Adult Years," in *Themes of Work and Love in Adulthood*, ed. by Smelser and Erikson, p. 213.

65. *Ibid.*, pp. 222–23.

66. *Ibid.*, p. 223.

67. Vaillant, *Adaptation to Life*, p. 338.

68. *Ibid.*, p. 339.

69. Levinson, *The Seasons of a Man's Life*, p. 334.

70. *Ibid.*, p. 333.

71. *Ibid.*, p. 147.

72. Alfred North Whitehead discusses the epistemological problem resulting from an increasingly complex world. See his *Process and Reality: An Essay in Cosmology* (New York: Macmillan, 1929) and *Adventures of Ideas* (New York: Macmillan, 1933); and also Paul W. Pruyser's discussion and use of Whitehead's position in *The Minister as Diagnostician: Personal Problems in Pastoral Perspective* (Philadelphia: Westminster Press, 1976), pp. 14–18, 80–81.

73. Pruyser, p. 58.

74. In addition to Pruyser's work, see Seward Hiltner, "Toward Autonomous Pastoral Diagnosis," *Bulletin of the Menninger Clinic*, 40 (1976), 573–92.

75. Burrell, p. 124.

76. W. W. Meissner, "Psychoanalytic Aspects of Religious Experience," *Annual of Psychoanalysis*, 6 (1978), 107–14.

CHAPTER THREE

Conversion and Discernment in Midlife

"Abbot Lot came to Abbot Joseph and said: 'Father, according as I am able, I keep my little rule, and my little fast, my prayer, meditation and contemplative silence; and according as I am able I strive to cleanse my heart of thoughts: now what more should I do?' The elder rose up in reply and stretched out his hands to heaven, and his fingers became like ten lamps of fire. He said: 'Why not be totally changed into fire?'"[1]

This little story from the monastic tradition of the fourth century Egyptian desert poignantly illustrates the unfinished quality of conversion even in the lives of the observant. St. Paul had earlier laid out the same idea: "Not that I have already obtained this or am already perfect; but I press on to make it my own, because Christ Jesus has made me his own. Brethren, I do not consider that I have made it my own; but one thing I do, forgetting what lies ahead, I press on toward the goal for the prize of the upward call of God in Christ Jesus" (Phil. 3:12–14).

The converting person is constantly leaving a past behind in order to be open for something more. Conversion requires a person to discern what is to be left behind and what is to be welcomed. Conversion and discernment are correlative activities. An analysis of these two processes will suggest various approaches to both the psychological and spiritual challenges of midlife. For directors, conversion and discernment can serve as key terms and as frames of reference for comprehending what people face at midlife.

Preludes to Conversion

The questioning of one's life and values, which is characteristic of midlife, is often a prelude to further conversion. To question is to distance oneself, to take a critical stance toward one's life. To question is to open oneself to change, to thinking and to acting differently. Jesus raised questions by telling parables; his stories about the loving father and prodigal son or the compassionate Samaritan were designed to unsettle. They were intended to invite people to take another look at their lives. They were calls to conversion. People in midlife can find in parables a challenge to change their perspectives on life. These unsettling stories support the process of reexamination which is often necessary for a successful negotiation of the midlife passage.

Parables can overturn a person's way of looking at life. "People resist parables because, subconsciously at least, they sense that their human-made world is being called into question by them; that should they pass over, be converted, to the world of the parable, take on its perspective in a radical and total way (and parables always demand a total response of heart, imagination, intellect, will, and life-style), nothing would ever again be the same."[2] Parables are stories which can shatter the very foundations of an accepted world. They challenge the conventional life stories people fashion for themselves, and they suggest new and different outcomes to ordinary life events.

Uneasiness with one's self and one's world at midlife is an opportunity for conversion of the deepest sort. Spiritual directors need to be sensitive to this. In some cases they should support the questioning which is already going on; in others cases they should create a situation where questions can emerge. The dis-ease which people feel can lead to spiritual and psychological well-being. Carl Jung has remarked: "We cannot live the afternoon of life according to the programme of life's morning—for what was great in the morning will be little at evening, and what in the morning was true will at evening have become a lie."[3] Direction should at times be uncomfortable. Since conversion changes a person's perspective on life, some disorientation and discomfort is unavoidable.

Taylor Caldwell in her novel *Bright Flows the River* describes a woman who vehemently fought against the questioning which can lead to conversion. "Mary's favorite word was 'comfortable.' It was not 'comfortable' to question where there was no answer, though, in truth, she did not fully know that there were no complete answers. . . .To accept was to be secure. Not to accept everything was to open yourself to danger and fear. She did not put these thoughts into words, for her mental vocabulary was very limited, but she felt them in her soul, and shivered."[4] Caldwell writes of the price Mary paid in maintaining her rigid position: "Wonder was alien to her, delight was incomprehensible, laughter was suspect, 'too much education' was effete. Work was her true god, and she totally believed that God labored without rest, and gloomily monitored His only world. A laughing God would have seemed blasphemous to her. She knew the cant that 'God is Love,' but she did not know the meaning."[5]

Mary is the mother of the novel's central figure, Guy Jerald. It is Guy who suffers a painful breakdown of the secure, comfortable world which Mary had helped him construct. Plunged into a deep depression, he struggles to come to a new acceptance of himself and of life. He breaks out of his confinement and discovers a reality which his mother never suspected. But his midlife crisis is severe. After he nearly kills himself, he is hospitalized and receives the ministry of a caring psychiatrist. Conversion to a fuller life meant a painful review of his past and courageous efforts to plot a new course. Yet the message of the novel is one of hope. "In the dark night of the soul, bright flows the river of God."[6]

Guy Jerald's conversion is not an explicitly religious event. In fact, it represents a repudiation of some of the religious and moral values which he had formerly espoused. Yet, in dying to his old self, he discovers an unknown dimension of depth in himself and in his life. He arrives at a stage which is totally different from Mary's and that of others like her. Conversion puts him more in touch with the truth of himself and the world.

Conversion and the Self

A director's awareness of movements toward conversion in a person's life can be an important factor in skilled direction. However, according to Walter E. Conn, "conversion remains one of the most widely used but least understood words in the religious vocabulary."[7] Fortunately, however, recent contributions of theologians and psychologists have focused on the multifaceted nature of conversion and have enabled directors to see the many spiritual and psychological tasks of midlife as integrally related one to another.

William James (1842–1910) was a pioneer in the psychological exploration of the nature of conversion. In *The Varieties of Religious Experience* (1902) James noted that in conversion previously peripheral ideas move to center stage within the stream of consciousness. These ideas then constitute a "hot place" in consciousness, a new center of energy, and they provide a new framework for organizing a multitude of experiences.[8] Conversion brings a sense of unification to those who have struggled with a feeling of inner division. "To be converted, to be regenerated, to receive grace, to experience religion, to gain an assurance are so many phrases which denote the process, gradual or sudden, by which a self hitherto divided, and consciously wrong, inferior and unhappy, becomes unified and consciously right, superior and happy, in consequence of its firmer hold upon religious realities."[9]

For James, conversion is a possible answer to those who experience the torment of a divided self. He contrasted this group with those whom he designated the "healthy-minded." The latter were people whose lives evolved smoothly without noticeable crisis. These were the "once-born" whose religious growth was a gradual process. With the divided selves, the "sick-minded," religious growth seemed the result of sudden conversion. James observes, "the sufferer, when saved, is saved by what seems to him as a second birth, a deeper kind of conscious being than he could enjoy before."[10]

James's typology of the healthy-minded and the sick-minded was based on the evidence he had on hand.[11] Although it is not exhaustive and is only intended to illustrate varieties of religious experience, this typology may well strike a responsive chord in the mind of directors. Certainly some people who come for direction at midlife would fit the category of the sick-minded; others would more properly belong in the category of healthy-minded, and these would present a different challenge to directors. In the direction of the sick-minded, James's observations on the divided self and conversion as a way out of this condition are illuminating.

The psychic condition of many people in contemporary society supports this insight about the divided self.[12] The major patterns of the divided self are found in people who are beset by lasting internal conflicts. These conflicts often pit a seemingly indispensable need for

59

love and esteem from important figures of childhood against a current need for independent thought and action. Loyalty to parents, for example, is challenged when something new and different is envisioned for the self. New beliefs about God, the world, and the self can call into question a person's fidelity to these trusted figures of the past. The experience is one of division; part of the person wants to maintain the loyalty, while another part strains to pull away. This is not an uncommon situation for persons at midlife. "The aroused feelings of shame and disloyalty can be borne only when they are counteracted by great gains in deeper satisfactions or when the new loyalty is directed to an altogether more worthy or admirable object who is felt to have a greater claim on the person's devotion."[13]

Another pattern of the divided self occurs in the conflict between rationality and basic drives. Good reason no longer easily prevails over pressing desires for instinctual gratification. A battle wages between realistic control and pleasurable impulse, and the will itself seems divided. The division can be experienced as a conflict between divergent beliefs such as the pure capriciousness of life, on the one hand, and God's providential direction of life, on the other.[14]

There may also be a war between a false self and the true self. A false self is often described as one of many possible public selves which has been fashioned for the sake of conformity to a social environment, and thus it stifles creative living.[15] Thomas Merton describes the struggle between the true self and a false self as part of the spiritual journey. In *New Seeds of Contemplation* he writes: "All sin starts from the assumption that my false self, the self that exists only in my own egocentric desires, is the fundamental reality of life to which everything else in the universe is ordered. Thus I use up my life in the desire for pleasures and the thirst for experiences, for power, honor, knowledge, and love to clothe this false self and construct its nothingness into something objectively real."[16] In contrast, "The true inner self, the true indestructible and immortal person, the true 'I' who answers to a new and secret name known only to himself and to God, does not 'have' anything, even 'contemplation'. This 'I' is not the kind of subject that can amass experiences, reflect on them, reflect on himself, for this 'I' is not the superficial and *empirical* self that we know in our everyday life."[17]

James regarded conversion as a possible source of healing for the divided self because of the opening out to a "wider self." "The further limits of our being plunge . . . into an altogether other dimension of existence from the sensible and merely 'understandable' world."[18] James suggested that sudden conversions are the result of subliminal mental work. This subliminal consciousness or the subconscious is a possible means of contact with an all-encompassing spiritual reality. In fact, James wondered if the subliminal, what is today called the unconscious, might not be the "hither side" of the something more which people call the holy. Speaking in terms of his own "over-beliefs," that is, in terms of intellectual beliefs and ideas which made sense to him, he observed: "We and God have business with each other; and in opening ourselves to his influence our deepest destiny is fulfilled. The universe, as those parts of it which our personal being constitutes, takes a turn genuinely for the worse or for the better in proportion as each one of us fulfills or evades God's demands."[19]

Conversion Moments

James's account of conversion experiences throws light upon the possibilities for healing the self and also upon the role played by the unconscious. This descriptive and interpretive endeavor, which has special relevance for directors who work with midlife adults, has been further advanced in the work of James Loder, *The Transforming Moment: Understanding Convictional Experiences.*[20] Loder's book is a call for people to take more seriously the often radical convictional experiences in which a person's ordinary ways of seeing and being in the world are transcended. "Transforming moments need to be recognized as sources of new knowledge about God, self, and the world, and as generating the quality and strength of life that can deal creatively with the sense of nothingness shrouding the extremities and pervading the mainstream of modern living."[21]

The new sense of reality which arises in these transforming moments includes an awareness of the void which threatens humanity, ultimately personal or collective death. But it moves beyond the void to recognize that which negates the threat—the holy. Whereas ordinary knowing is two-dimensional, focusing on the self and the world, the knowledge which emerges from convictional experiences is four-dimensional, incorporating the void and the holy as well. What is helpful for skilled spiritual direction is Loder's analysis of this transformational knowing which comes as the result of a five part process.

Transformational knowing begins in an experience of conflict when previous ways of knowing begin to break down. It is a phenomenon similar to that which confronts a person who is trying to solve a puzzle. When attempts at solving the puzzle based on one's usual interpretative schemes fail, the *second* step finds people scanning the field of possibilities for a new perspective while they continue to be challenged by the conflict. This scanning, which relies heavily on the imagination, is both a conscious and an unconscious process. *Thirdly*, an intuition or insight which gives a clue to the resolution of the conflict appears on the boundary between the unconscious and the conscious as a result of a constructive act of the imagination. "It is by this central act that the elements of the ruptured situation are *transformed*, and a new perception, perspective, or world view is bestowed on the knower."[22] With the appearance of the insight, the knower experiences a surge of energy—energy which was formerly absorbed by the conflict. Release from the conflict in this *fourth* step gives rise to self-transcendence. The new insight makes possible *finally* a reinterpretation of the problem situation. A new vision is applied to the former conflict and to a corresponding world view.

Loder shows that the pattern of transformational knowing is operative in areas as diverse as education, therapy, art, and scientific discovery. In every case an imaginative leap brings about a resolution of a conflict situation.

At midlife, the puzzle or conflict situation which faces people often presents itself in the form of the self torn between boundless desires and inescapable limits. Allen Wheelis in his autobiographical novel, *The Scheme of Things*, points to the confusion that results: "We are, all of us . . . in a maze and lost. We follow now this lead, now another, veer this way and that through corridors of anguish, boredom, and—oh, so rarely!—joy. What are we up to? Where are we going? To what purpose? Occasionally we glimpse a phantom vision, gone in a flicker. I search for an informing principle. I want a truth that will teach us how to live, will define our task, will enable us to become fully human, to use ourselves up in a way that counts. A life so lived should then verify the principle that directed it."[23] However, it takes a heroic individual to face creaturely limitations, experience contradiction, and still retain a passion for life. "Who knows what form the forward momentum of life will take in the time ahead or what use it will make of our anguished searching. The most that any one of us can seem to do is to fashion something—an object or ourselves—and drop it into the confusion, make an offering of it, so to speak, to the life force."[24] That, in turn, requires courage. The limits and the contradictions must be faced, for "the creative act arises out of the struggle of human beings with and against that which limits them."[25]

According to Loder's schema, transformational knowing takes place in a therapeutic relationship between two people when a "therapist" offers support so that a "client" can courageously face his or her conflict, scan for a resolution, and bring about a creative act whereby the self comes to be known in a new way. "The surest sign that healing has occurred in therapeutic knowing is the freedom of the "I" to choose for the self and against patterns of self-destruction."[26] Spiritual direction results in a similar type of knowing. Moreover, Loder's remarks about the void and the holy are especially pertinent for direction.

The void can be experienced as absence, loneliness, shame, guilt, hatred, the demonic, or death. It comes into clear view when a person's world begins to break apart in the experience of some conflict: life's order is shattered. In Joseph Conrad's *Heart of Darkness*, Marlow, a man in midlife, undertakes a journey into the heart of Africa. As he recalls the beginning of his voyage, he remarks: "For a time I would feel I belonged still to a world of straightforward facts; but the feeling would not last long. Something would turn up to scare it away. . . . It was like a weary pilgrimage amongst hints for nightmares."[27]

But there is something more than the threat of the void. In a convictional experience the face of the void is negated and transformed into the face of God. At these times a person is brought face to face with the graciousness of being itself, and by finding his or her self grounded in its very source it realizes that its true nature is to be a self that gives love. "The essence of convictional knowing is the intimacy of the self with its Source. The breakdown of the eternal distance between them, the establishment of the internal dialogue, the illumination of Christ, the shared joy of Christ and the thrust into the people and culture of Christ, together constitute the shape of that intimacy. This is the form of the ongoing spiritual communion into which convictional experiences call the believer, not once but again and again throughout life."[28]

Convictional knowing is experienced as a gift from the all-gracious God. The conversion it accomplishes is a radical recentering on God. Those who courageously face the void of loss, abandonment, and death open themselves to this gift. Loder indicates that in the course of any human development the transformational process can be seen at work. The stages of development bring people time and time again to a breakdown of a secure world of their own and society's making. Just as the infant brings order into chaos by the discovery of its mother's face, humanity longs for the face which will transform the void of human loneliness.

Faith, Conversion, and Adult Development

Through religious conversion some people find answers to questions which have been with them throughout their lives. They discover a God who responds to the longings of the human heart and who provides a sense of wholeness. They also discover a transcendent goal for the self, which unifies it and moves it beyond its merely empirical dimension. Often in the events surrounding this conversion, the questions themselves change and a long cherished religious faith is challenged. As the adult person develops, new issues come to the fore and new questions are put to the faith which has sustained the person thus far. Suffering and death, easily kept at arm's length in youth, begin to press in on an individual's personal space at midlife, and they raise penetrating questions, often in a dramatic way.

In his book, *The Stages of Faith: The Psychology of Human Development and the Quest for Meaning*, James Fowler recounts such an experience which had a dramatic effect on him. "Four A.M., in the darkness of a cold winter morning, suddenly I am fully and frighteningly awake. I see it clearly: I am going to die. *I* am going to die. This body, this mind, this lived and living myth, this husband, father, teacher, son, friend, will cease to be. . . . In the strange aloneness of this moment, defined by the certainty of death, I awake to the true facts of life."[29] Fowler mentions questions which surfaced at that time: "As never before, I found myself asking, 'When all these persons and relations and projects that shape and fill my life are removed, who or what is left? . . . What continuities will there be between these full, fleeting days and years I now taste and savor and any enlargement of time I may experience?' "[30]

Building upon experiences such as this one, in his structural-developmental study of faith, Fowler understands *faith* as a universal human capacity to relate to a transcendent dimension of life. As such, it is to be distinguished from *belief* which has as its object a conceptual or propositional rendering of an experience or relationship to the transcendent.

Faith is rather a process of knowing and valuing, a dynamic activity which creates and sustains an organizing frame of meaning for life. Faith provides a "dependable life space" in which persons find meaning and order for human existence. It does this through imaging an "ultimate environment," an outer boundary to all that goes on in life. "Faith, in its binding us to centers of value and power and in its triadic joining of us into communities of shared trusts and loyalties, gives form and content to our imaging of an ultimate environment. . . . Faith, as imagination, grasps the ultimate conditions of our existence, unifying them into a comprehensive image in light of which we shape our responses and initiatives, our actions."[31] A symbol such as the Kingdom of God gives outward expression to faith's way of imaging an ultimate environment. Symbols and images enable people to sustain trusting relationships.

Following the work of Jean Piaget, Erik Erikson, and Lawrence Kohlberg in cognitive, psychosocial, and moral development respectively, Fowler proposes a stage theory of faith development. He observes: "The images faith composes are not static. By virtue of our research and observation I believe that we can identify reasonably predictable developmental turning points in the *ways* faith imagines and in the ways faith's images interplay with communal modes of expression."[32] Based on data gathered from interviews, the stage sequence of faith development gives us insights into the typical changes people experience in faith-imaging as they mature. Complemented with Loder's explanation of transforming moments, this scheme can point out many of the features people can expect to experience on the journey of faith.

Directors of midlife adults will find Fowler's remarks about the ordinary development of faith helpful in their work. However, a few words of caution are in order. A possible conclusion from Fowler's theory is that there is one ideal stage of faith for everyone. The notion of progress is implicit in his theory, and hence a sense that later stages are better than earlier ones. Such value judgments should be avoided. Although Fowler himself holds that the stage sequence is a normative and a multifaceted approach to faith, directors would do well to approach it simply as an insightful and useful descriptive scheme for understanding the development of the cognitive dimension of faith.[33] Viewed in this way, the theory suggests different ways of thinking about midlife struggles and conversion.

Fowler's description of conjunctive faith, for example, highlights significant dimensions of a transformation of faith at midlife. This pattern of faith is best considered, however, in the context of the other stages. Transitions from one stage to another are occasioned by new experiences, new ways of knowing, and by changes in environment. Each stage is a relatively stable pattern of faith, which is characterized by particular forms of knowing, thinking, and valuing.

In Fowler's system there is a pre-stage of undifferentiated faith at the beginnings of life. He relates this faith to the issue of trust versus mistrust which Erikson sees as the first developmental crisis a person faces. Stage I emerges by the age of two; this is an intuitive-projective faith characterized by powerful images around which the world of experience is unified. With continued psychosocial maturation and cognitive development, a mythic-literal faith, stage II, makes its appearance around the age of seven when narrative becomes important for giving coherence to experience. Stage III, a synthetic-conventional faith, is an attempt to understand the ultimate environment in interpersonal terms. This stage has its ascendancy in adolescence when a person is concerned with establishing identity. As a move toward a coherent worldview in terms of which one learns to understand the self and others, it is a conformist stage. Though characteristic of the adolescent, this stage of faith development may be the last reached by some adults.

With the advent of young adulthood, an individuative-reflective faith, stage IV, comes into prominence. This faith has the characteristics of critical reflection on identity and worldview which young adults typically engage in. Less dependent on authority, these people now make their own judgments and formulate a coherent worldview which makes sense to them. Symbols are translated into conceptual meanings and a multi-layered reality is often simplified for the sake of comprehensibility.

At midlife unconscious forces begin to intrude into carefully ordered existences, and this sets the stage for a transition to stage V. Fowler first referred to this stage as paradoxical-consolidative faith, but more recently he has designated it conjunctive faith. Much of what was overlooked in stage IV now begins to be incorporated. Symbols are appreciated for the depths of meaning they point to as well as for their conceptual meaning. In the language of Paul Ricoeur, the new openness to the symbolic represents a "second naïveté," a movement beyond the critical reflection of the previous stage while not negating the gains of that stage. Fowler speaks of "the rise of the ironic imagination—a capacity to see and be in one's or one's group's most powerful meanings, while simultaneously recognizing that they are relative, partial and inevitably distorting apprehensions of transcendent reality."[34]

Conjunctive faith implies a new acquisition of personal identity which is more open to the unconscious depths of the person. It involves coming to terms with personal history, reclaiming overlooked parts of that history, and reworking the understanding of the whole. With it comes a willingness to meet reality on its own terms and a more ardent pursuit of a multifaceted truth. Paradox and apparent contradictions are not only tolerated but are now seen as necessary dimensions of a true vision of reality. People possessing a conjunctive faith work for the reconciliation of opposites in themselves. They strive for unity in the social sphere but lack the unifying vision given to those at stage VI.

Universalizing faith is the designation Fowler gives to stage VI. He feels that few achieve this level of faith development. "The rare persons who may be described by this stage have a special grace that makes them seem more lucid, more simple, and yet somehow more fully human than the rest of us. Their community is universal in extent. . . . Such persons are ready for fellowship with persons at any of the other stages and from any other faith tradition."[35]

Some people in direction at midlife will exhibit the characteristics of a faith stage transition. Directors may observe that some are moving from a synthetic-conventional faith to an individuative-reflective faith. Others will exhibit the movement Fowler ascribes to the midlife period, a transition from an individuative-reflective faith to a conjunctive faith. This latter movement is often prompted by a person's awareness of new inner stirrings. As people begin to open up to their own unconscious and discover a depth in themselves which was previously unnoticed, there seems to be a natural turning to symbolic language to describe what is happening within.

Directors can be supportive of this transition in faith. Fowler highlights the importance of sponsors and sponsoring communities for ongoing faith development. It is very important for people to have an opportunity to put into words their experience of a changing faith orientation. Fowler's remarks on sponsorship bear directly on spiritual direction: "The sponsor is one who walks with you; one who knows the path and can provide guidance. The sponsor is one who engenders trust and proves trustworthy in supporting you in difficult passages or turns. The sponsor may, as needed, confront you, insisting that difficult issues be faced and that self-deceptions or sloth be avoided. The sponsor or sponsoring community should be able to provide both models and experiences in education and spiritual direction that deepen and expand one's initial commitments and provide the nurture for strong and continuing growth."[36]

Fowler is more interested in the evolving structures of faith rather than in the contents of faith. Conversion, for him, refers properly to changes in faith's contents—centers of value, images of power, and master stories. He specifies conversion as "a significant recentering of one's previous conscious or unconscious images of value and power, and the conscious adoption of a new set of master stories in the commitment to reshape one's life in a new community of interpretation and action."[37] A stage transition, a change in the structure of faith, may accompany or precipitate conversion. Conversion likewise may precipitate stage change or possibly block it.

For direction, conversion is best seen as encompassing both the structural and the content changes of faith. Midlife experience will lead some people to a structural shift in faith, others to a deeper understanding of the content of faith or even to new content, and still others to changes in both structure *and* content. The role of the director is not to induce a movement to the next faith stage but rather to facilitate conversion as a life-long process. Attention to process will focus the energy of those in direction on the Other who invites and on their own fuller response to that invitation. As such, direction does not neglect the human dimensions of faith, but it gives central attention to the divine initiative in ongoing faith development and conversion.

People in direction are encouraged to allow faith to color the whole of their lives. This is an aspect of ongoing conversion, the process side of faith. Winston Gooden has spoken of attention to this process dimension as faith-work: "the continuous integrative shaping of one's life in accordance with the overarching framework of meaning one has chosen."[38] Faith-work includes a process of integration, formation, and transformation.

The integration side of faith-work refers to the efforts a person makes to broaden self-identity by including more aspects of life and the self. Even the shadow side of the personality, which Jung has described in detail, becomes more clearly related to a person's faith vision. This is especially relevant to midlife individuation. In *The Undiscovered Self* Jung comments: "What our age thinks of as the 'shadow' and inferior part of the psyche contains more than something merely negative. The very fact that through self-knowledge, i.e., by exploring our own souls, we come upon the instincts and their world of imagery should throw some light on the powers slumbering in the psyche, of which we are seldom aware so long as all goes well. They are potentialities of the greatest dynamism, and it depends entirely on the preparedness and attitude of the conscious mind whether the irruption of these forces and the images and ideas associated with them will tend towards construction or catastrophe."[39]

Midlife dealings with the shadow side of the personality can be the occasion for the transforming moments which Loder has described. A new faith perception of reality can also occur, since there is a close correlation between faith and self-identity. When the self is accepted with its limits, a deeper relationship to God as the object of faith is made possible. Jung observed that all human relationships are solidly established when there is a recognition of imperfection. "The perfect has no need of the other, but weakness has, for it seeks support and does not confront its partner with anything that might force him into an inferior position and even humiliate him."[40]

Formation, what Gooden calls a shaping process, is the second aspect of faith-work. Here the framework of faith is taken seriously for directing, organizing, and giving meaning to one's life. Formation implies consciously deciding to let faith predominate over other factors which vie for a controlling influence over one's life. Midlife individuals may find themselves struggling to be steadfast in decisions which they made earlier in their lives. Directors sometimes help these people by pointing out the dissonances between their chosen faith orientation and their daily living.

When the framework of meaning which faith has provided proves inadequate, a process of transformation is required. This is the third aspect of faith-work. Transformation involves reworking the framework of meaning. The Dark Night experience described by John of the Cross calls for just such a change in framework. The darkness and desolation are "reframed" and seen anew as experiences of God. Transformations of this sort are often required in midlife transitions along with the integration side of faith-work.

Gooden notes the value of outside assistance in times of transition for sustaining an individual in difficult faith-work. "Persons who understand or have gone through a mid-life crisis may be able to shepherd others experiencing a similar crisis by facilitating the doubting, disillusioning, and questioning. . . . The guide, by being there, can enable the transitioner to face and work through these dark experiences and give comfort as well as insight."[41] Directors, however, must not try to formulate a program for an individual's conversion at midlife. Stage theory may illuminate what takes place in a person's faith development, and the three aspects of faith-work may indicate what needs to be done, but conversion is more than simply human work and development. Christian faith maintains that conversion occurs in response to a divine initiator, whose advents into people's lives cannot be programmed. Surrender to that divine Other is conversion of the highest order. To help a person discern the presence of the Other in their life means, above all, to allow that person the autonomy they need to be open to the experience of conversion.

Discernment and the Conversion Process

Ideally the Christian life is an ongoing conversion process, and the process is often facilitated by the questions which midlife presents to people. By stepping aside from their usual way of looking at things, people expose themselves to situations of vulnerability. Once the safe, secure homelands are left behind, they experience crises. In the light of New Testament teaching, these are times for making judgments and being judged. Erikson has spoken of crisis as a time of increased potential and heightened vulnerability. It is also a time of disorientation; it is often depicted as an encounter with death. Religious people are frequently driven to admit that God becomes their only refuge.

Thus, the journey of conversion is a frightening one, despite the numerous testimonies to favorable outcomes. As a journey, the conversion process finds an echo in stage theory which points out some way stations along the road. For Christians the way has been shown in Jesus, whose life is a paradigm for the conversion process. In his life, moreover, ongoing conversion is coupled with ongoing discernment.

The Jesus of the Gospels pursued the will of the Father as his ongoing conversion. For Jesus the Father's will went beyond the limits of what was already known as good. The will of the Father was something new that he had to be and had to do. In his human consciousness, the task of discerning this will involved clarifying for himself who God really was. This meant discerning the ever greater reality of the God who comes in new ways and is not confined to rigidly fixed categories. Jesus demonstrated in his life that God was always more than the tradition about him had claimed.[42] Conversion and discernment together implied a radical openness to this greater God. From this standpoint the account of the temptations of Jesus are a dialogue between Jesus and the Father about who Jesus was to be before this ever greater God and how he, Jesus, was to do the right thing. Jesus' discernments led him to embrace a life of solidarity with the poor and the oppressed. His life was one of radical love—a love that does justice.

Jesus' life presented discernment as leading to radical choices between alternatives. People are to choose between God and mammon, life and death. They are to say yes to what God affirms in history and no to what God refutes as a world of sin. These choices flow from preliminary or foundational discernments of who God is and who people are in relation to God. As Jon Sobrino has remarked: "From Jesus we learn not so much the replies to our discernments as,

71

more basically, how to learn to discern. We learn this not so much by analyzing the internal psychology of Jesus in his process of discernment, but on the basis of the choices and historical commitments that Jesus made."[43]

The structure of Jesus' discernment can give shape and form to the quest of midlife persons who search for what they should be and do. Certainly the choice between alternatives which Jesus presents has been the focus of discernment for Christians throughout the centuries. Furthermore, the discernment of Jesus draws attention to the importance for a foundational discernment regarding God and self. Such foundational discernments develop over the course of a life. "The fact that God is greater," Sobrino observes, "did not come to Jesus from the momentary consideration of his transcendence, but through the process and praxis of his love. This is why his life not only went through different chronological stages but also through different theological stages; and why we should speak of a 'conversion' of Jesus, since he did not absolutize or validate forever the particular form of building the kingdom and responding to the Father that he saw in the first of his life."[44]

Discernment and Choices

The close connection between the lifelong processes of conversion and discernment is amply supported in the Christian tradition of spirituality. In chapter 72 of the sixth-century *Rule of Benedict*, monks are presented with two paths which are characterized as two different types of zeal: "Just as there is a wicked zeal of bitterness which separates from God and leads to hell, so there is a good zeal which separates from evil and leads to God and everlasting life."[45] The *Rule* describes in some detail the good effects in community life which result from individuals following the way of good zeal in their own personal lives.

Read against the background of the whole document as well as the earlier monastic tradition, this passage in the *Rule of Benedict* suggests a way of life in which there is an ongoing conversion which leads toward a community formed and animated by the love of Christ. In other words, the choices to be made by the monks are seen in a relational context. Some choices will contribute to the upbuilding of community; others will tear at the fabric of the community. In any case, the privatizing tendency of some spiritualities and much of contemporary human potential literature is absent.

The focus on good and evil zeal echoes the Gospel notion of "crisis" or choices between radical alternatives. For people today good zeal and evil zeal refer to the persistent conflict between outgoing love and selfish glibness. For midlife adults the tension can be described in terms of a struggle between generative care and narcissistic stagnation. The *Rule* not only points out this paradigmatic conflict in the human spirit but also suggests ways of overcoming it. The *Rule* is a religious classic, one of the many sources in the Christian tradition which can guide directors in their work.[46]

The choice between good zeal and evil zeal is not always easy and obvious. One needs discernment in this process to distinguish between the sources of one's motivation. The belief that underlies this approach to discernment is that the Lord directs people to ever deeper experience of his presence through their walking in the way of good zeal. The exhortatory parts of the *Rule* appeal directly to each one's motives as they call for an openness to the presence of the risen Lord in the community. "What, dear brothers, is more delightful than this voice of the Lord calling to us? See how the Lord in his love shows us the way of life. Clothed then with faith and the performance of good works, let us set out on this way, with the Gospel for our guide, that we may deserve to see him who has called us to his kingdom."[47] At special moments the brothers become aware of the Lord's presence as a consoling knowledge of God. The experience is a gift. It cannot be forced to come or come again. All the individual can do is to live in a way which does not prevent this openness.

To act with discernment is to leave the door open to experiences "of the Lord." This approach to living requires listening and pondering of all one's attitudes and experiences in the light of those incisive experiences of God's presence. The result is that life becomes directed; it is thrust in the direction which such experiences indicate. What is relevant here to the midlife struggle is a shift away from the self and an overcoming of narcissistic propensities as one makes a decided effort to seek the Lord and respond to him. This means that the response occurs in a relational context; the spiritual welfare of a community becomes a norm for an authentic response. Stagnation is overcome when discernment guides a person in an ongoing conversion process.

73

Discernment and Feelings

Discernment as an integral part of conversion is further supported by the *Spiritual Exercises* of Ignatius Loyola (1491–1556). As in the *Rule of Benedict*, discernment for Ignatius takes place in an atmosphere of prayer. Ignatius proposed two sets of rules for the discernment of spirits. In the first set a person seeks to discern with regard to choices between good and evil. In the second set the focus is on choices a person has to make between two goods. The aim throughout the *Exercises* is conversion which leads to appropriate resolutions regarding the future.[48]

The process of discernment requires a person to pay attention to the feelings which surface when various choices are considered. Ignatius spoke especially of consolation and desolation as the feelings to be aware of. "Ignatius came to recognize that human experiences of joy and desolation, of enthusiasm and depression, of light and darkness, are not just human emotions which vary like the wind in a storm, but are the means by which we recognize the movements within our spirit stirred by the Spirit of Jesus."[49]

By taking note of their feelings, people can come to the deep, affective self-knowledge which is essential for conversion. Though the self which persons come to know is a self that experiences conflict between reality and desires, this knowing process is not an exercise in self-absorption. "Ignatius' aim in the early exercises was to destroy a certain psychological preoccupation with oneself as saint or sinner. Ignatius desired exercitants to find the place of true sin and sinfulness within themselves whence true penance could arise, rather than to reinforce false idealizations and expectations which cut them off from their concrete history."[50]

A comprehensive self-knowledge is the goal. This knowledge comes through discovery of all parts of the self created and sustained by God, in short, the true self. The *Exercises* grew out of Ignatius's own efforts to come to know himself and God. In his quest he experienced intense emotional crises, and so he exemplifies the difficulties in any midlife journey toward deep self-knowledge. Through careful attention to his feelings, Ignatius was able to discern a direction for the future and make a radical life choice. For other people at midlife, a similar attention to their feelings can be the basis for sound discernment regarding their own conversions.

The choice which results from a discernment process like this is different from one which would emerge from a purely rational process. The foundation for the discernment process which Ignatius describes is an experience of God. Ignatius calls it a "consolation without a previous cause."[51] In an essay on the underlying theology of the Ignatian rules for discernment, Karl Rahner describes this consolation as "an experiencing of the complete openness of the soul to all being, the limitless capacity of the mind to know all things knowable, its 'transcendence' or an ability to go beyond any particular limited object, as now directed toward its limitless limit, God himself."[52]

Concrete choices are then to be made on the basis of a consoling and gifted experience of God's presence. "It is a process of experiment and trial, to see whether the direction in which the possible choice leads the exercitant can be synthesized with his fundamental religious experience of complete openness to God."[53] Such an experience of God presupposes that an individual has achieved a detachment from lesser objects. As Rahner notes, "the only person who can really choose freely is the person who by the grace of God . . . has been liberated from the enslaving tyranny of intramundane 'principalities and powers,' that is, from the unbelieving illusion that, in order to exist, man must absolutize something in the world of existential experience."[54]

Dying to the false self and learning how to deal with inordinate attachments are prerequisites for a fuller response to the God who invites people to deeper experiences of his presence. Spiritual direction seeks to facilitate these experiences by uncovering the obstacles to greater openness to that presence. Direction cannot, however, be adequately understood apart from the grace which enables people to overcome the blindness they have about their own falsity. Welcoming and cooperating with grace leads a person to a clearer vision of what needs to be done in the ongoing conversion of their life. Sound judgments can be made on the basis of this clearer vision.

Discernment, Judgment, and Interpretation

Discernment has been closely connected with making judgments both in the tradition of Christian spirituality and in recent theology. John Cassian (c. 360–435) viewed the discerning person as a "prudent money-changer" who carefully judged between genuine spiritual thoughts and earthly ones. Cassian saw thoughts as having their origin in God, in the devil, or in the self. "We ought then carefully to notice this threefold order, and with a wise discretion to analyse the thoughts which arise in our hearts, tracking out their origin and cause and author in the first instance, that we may be able to consider how to yield ourselves to them in accordance with desert of those who suggest them, so that we may, as the Lord's command bids us, become good money-changers."[55]

Earlier St. Paul had listed the ability to distinguish between spirits among the spiritual gifts (1 Cor 12:10). Writers who followed Paul spoke of "discernment of spirits," those good and devil spirits which can influence people.[56] In *The Life of Antony*, St. Athanasius attributes the following words to that first of a long line of monks: "Much prayer and asceticism is needed so that one who receives through the Spirit the gift of discrimination might be able to recognize [the evil spirits'] traits—for example, which of them are less wicked, and which more; and in what kind of pursuit each of them exerts himself, and how each of them is overturned and expelled."[57]

For Cassian, however, the spirits are not separate entities that beset people, but they rise up within people's hearts. The discerning person possesses good judgment and walks the way of moderation in all things. "You see then that the gift of [discernment] is no earthly thing and no slight matter, but the greatest prize of divine grace. And unless a monk has pursued it with all zeal, and secured a power of discerning with unerring judgment the spirits that rise up in him, he is sure to go wrong. . . ."[58] For Cassian this unerring discernment is a gift which is secured by humility, especially in the willingness to submit all things to the scrutiny of the elders.

The struggle a person may have with conflicting desires at midlife may offer an opportunity for discernment of spirits in Cassian's sense. These spirits can be thought of as good zeal versus evil zeal or as the conflicting forces of creativity and destruction. Impulses toward full human growth must be distinguished from those forces, however they may be disguised as good, which lead a person toward stagnation. An analogy can be drawn between these conflicting interior movements and the forces of entropy and evolution in the natural sphere.[59] Entropy describes the tendency of systems to run down or to move from states of greater differentiation to states of lesser differentiation. Evolution is a movement toward more refined adaptation and organization. In pursuing their own spiritual growth, people face the powerful opposition of possible decline and fragmentation, the consequences of spiritual entropy.

In *The Road Less Traveled*, M. Scott Peck has described this force of entropy in a person's life as laziness.[60] He suggests that it be countered by the fostering of greater awareness. People who become aware of their own laziness have taken the first step toward overcoming it. This laziness can take many forms. Some people experience it as a fear of what will be expected of them if they continue to develop. In spiritual direction this laziness often shows up as an unwillingness to examine how one looks at oneself and at God. This tendency to remain locked into a particular way of viewing life and viewing God leads to stagnation.

Spiritual direction, on the other hand, fosters the dynamic aspects of life. By encouraging and assisting discernment, directors try to unmask the demonic wherever it is found. Sustained by God's gracious power, discerning individuals become aware of their subtle self-deceptions and are enabled to make sound judgments about their true state of affairs. They can interpret accurately, respond to life situations in a healthy manner, and then begin to plot a realistic course for the future.

Consequently, discernment has an important place in Christian moral theology; it plays a prominent role in decision-making.[61] The criteria a person may use to evaluate moral choices are found in the central symbols of the Christian tradition and in the basic virtues of the Christian life, such as radical dependence on God and repentance. Discernment, however, engages persons holistically, in their feelings, memories, and imaginings. Within the framework of general moral principles, discernment helps people to make specific judgments about moral actions which are consistent with their graced life stories and consistent with their community's tradition of acting in response to God's call.

In the spiritual tradition, discernment has always focused on God's action in a person's life and on what an appropriate response to God's action should be. For the person at midlife, the question is often "What is God's invitation to me at this point in my life?" In some cases the task is to discern God's call in what appears to be a desert. In others cases it is a matter of ascertaining whether the perceived "call" is from God or is merely self-deception. The response also has to be considered: "How is this call to be heeded, or how can this deception be dispelled?"

Sandra Schneiders has spoken about three different but related types of judgment which are involved in the discernment process.[62] The first of these is an *evaluative* judgment in which some determination is made about the truth or falsity of a phenomenon such as the perception of a call to change. This is followed by a second judgment, a *hermeneutical* one, in which some interpretation of the phenomenon is achieved. Finally, there is a *practical* judgment in which an appropriate response is formulated.

In direction at midlife, the issues of interpretation have special importance. Hermeneutical judgments can help a person to discover their true self and center it in God. Through interpretation deeper levels of meaning in a person's life are revealed. As Schneiders remarks, "discernment is the ability to see the revelatory meaning in the ongoing process of one's own or another's life, to see, as the saints say, 'with the eyes of faith' the salvific significance of what seem to be ordinary events."[63] In the next chapter hermeneutical theory relevant to the work of directors will be presented in relation to the task of interpreting the images of God and self and the stories of people at midlife.

Notes to Chapter Three

1. *The Wisdom of the Desert: Sayings from the Desert Fathers of the Fourth Century,* trans. by Thomas Merton (New York: New Directions, 1960), p. 50.

2. Sallie McFague, "Conversion: Life on the Edge of the Raft," *Interpretation,* 32 (1978), 257. See also John Dominic Crossan, *The Dark Interval: Towards a Theology of Story* (Niles, Ill.: Argus, 1975).

3. *Modern Man in Search of a Soul,* p. 108.

4. (New York: Fawcett Crest, 1978), p. 82.

5. *Ibid.,* pp. 83–4.

6. *Ibid.,* p. 509.

7. "Conversion: A Developmental Perspective," *Cross Currents,* 32 (1982), 323.

8. (New York: Collier Books, 1961), pp. 160–66. See Gary T. Alexander, "Psychological Foundations of William James's Theory of Religious Experience," *Journal of Religion,* 59 (1979), 425–428.

9. James, p. 160.

10. *Ibid.,* p. 135.

11. See James E. Dittes's comments on a correct reading of James in his "Beyond William James" in *Beyond the Classics: Essays in the Scientific Study of Religion,* ed. by C. Y. Glock and Philip Hammond (New York: Harper & Row, 1973), p. 299–302.

12. This section follows Paul Pruyser's discussion of the divided self and contemporary individuals in *Between Belief and Unbelief* (New York: Harper & Row, 1974), pp. 132–36.

13. *Ibid.,* pp. 138–39.

14. *Ibid.,* pp. 136–37.

15. See D. W. Winnicott, "Ego Distortion in Terms of True and False Self" in *The Maturational Processes and the Facilitating Environment* (New York: International Universities Press, 1965), pp. 140–52.

16. (New York: New Directions, 1961), pp. 34–35.

17. *Ibid.,* p. 279. Merton's description of the discovery of the true self is studied in James Finley, *Merton's Place of Nowhere: A Search for God Through Awareness of the True Self* (Notre Dame, Ind.: Ave Maria, 1978).

18. James, p. 399.

19. *Ibid.,* pp. 399–400. See James Forsyth, "Psychology, Theology, and William James," *Soundings,* 65 (1982), 402–16.

20. (San Francisco, Harper & Row, 1981). Writing out of the Protestant tradition, Loder is reluctant to use the term "conversion" because of its close linkage with emotionalism. He finds the theological synonym "metanoia" more palatable but still opts for the term "convictional experience" as most expressive of the radical alteration of a person's way of looking at the world and self which he wants to study.

21. Loder, p. viii.

22. *Ibid.*, p. 33.

23. (New York: Harcourt Brace Jovanovich, 1980), pp. 26–27.

24. Ernest Becker, *The Denial of Death* (New York: Free Press, 1973), p. 285.

25. Rollo May, *The Courage to Create* (New York: Bantam, 1976), p. 135.

26. Loder, p. 60.

27. *Heart of Darkness and The Secret Sharer* (New York: New American Library, 1910), pp. 78–79; see Puzon, "The *Bildungsroman* of Middle Life," p. 9.

28. Loder, p. 123.

29. (San Francisco: Harper & Row, 1981), p. xi.

30. *Ibid.*

31. *Ibid.*, pp. 24–25.

32. *Ibid.*, p. 30.

33. For critical evaluations of Fowler's theory, see Kenneth Stokes, ed. *Faith Development in the Adult Life Cycle* (New York: W. H. Sadlier, 1982), especially the following essays: Winston Gooden, "Responses from An Adult Development Perspective," pp. 84–119; Gabriel Moran, "Responses from the Religious Education Perspective," pp. 149–77; and Robert Wuthnow, "A Sociological Perspective on Faith Development," pp. 209–43. This volume contains essays originally delivered at a Symposium on Faith Development in the Adult Life Cycle held at the College of St. Thomas in St. Paul, Minnesota. Evaluations of *Stages of Faith* by Margaret Gorman, Harvey D. Egan, Catherine M. Going, and Paul J. Philibert as well as a response to these critiques by Fowler are found in a review symposium in *Horizons*, 9 (1982), 104–26. An earlier critique of Fowler's work is Alfred McBride's "Reaction to Fowler: Fears About Procedure" in *Values and Moral Development*, ed. by Thomas C. Hennessy (New York: Paulist Press, 1976), pp. 211–18.

34. Fowler, p. 198.

35. *Ibid.*, p. 201.

36. *Ibid.*, p. 287; see also Fowler's essay, "Faith and the Structuring of Meaning" in *Toward Moral and Religious Maturity*, ed. by James W. Fowler and Antoine Vergote (Morristown, N.J.: Silver Burdett, 1980), esp. pp. 79–84.

37. *Stages of Faith*, p. 281–82. See James Loder's comments on Fowler's efforts to relate stage development to conversion in James E. Loder and James W. Fowler, "Conversations on Fowler's *Stages of Faith* and Loder's *The Transforming Moment*," *Religious Education*, 77 (1982), 134–135.

38. "Responses and Comments from an Adult Development Perspective" in Stokes, p. 101.

39. Translated by R. F. C. Hull (New York: New American Library, 1957/8), p. 119.

40. *Ibid.*, p. 117.

41. Gooden, p. 103.

42. See Jon Sobrino, "Following Jesus as Discernment," *Concilium*, 119 (1978), 14–24.

43. *Ibid.*, p. 18.

44. *Ibid.*, p. 20.

45. *RB 1980: The Rule of St. Benedict in Latin and English with Notes*, ed. by Timothy Fry *et al.* (Collegeville, Minn.: Liturgical Press, 1981), p. 293; see Ambrose Wathen, "The Exigencies of Benedict's Little Rule for Beginners— RB 72," *American Benedictine Review*, 29 (1978), 41–66 for a detailed study of the meaning of zeal in the *Rule*.

46. For the notion of the classic see Hans-Georg Gadamer, *Truth and Method* (New York: Continuum Publishing Company, 1975), pp. 253–58; and David Tracy, *The Analogical Imagination: Christian Theology and the Culture of Pluralism* (New York: Crossroad, 1981), pp. 193–202.

47. Prol. 19–21, *RB 1980*, p. 161; see Augusta Raabe, "Discernment of Spirits in the Prologue to the *Rule* of Benedict," *American Benedictine Review*, 23 (1972), 397–423 on which this section is dependent.

48. The literature on the *Spiritual Exercises* is immense. References are provided in Paul Begheyn, "A Bibliography on St. Ignatius' Spiritual Exercises: A Working Tool for American Students," *Studies in the Spirituality of Jesuits*, 13, no. 2 (1981). For a good introduction and translation of the *Exercises*, see *The Spiritual Exercises of St. Ignatius*, trans. by Anthony Mottola with an Introduction by Robert W. Gleason (Garden City, N.Y.: Doubleday, 1964). For the connection between Ignatius' teaching and the monastic tradition, see Heinrich Bacht, "Benedikt und Ignatius" in *Benedikt und Ignatius*, ed. by T. Bogler (Maria Laach, 1963), pp. 9–30; and *idem*, "Early Monastic Elements in Ignatian Spirituality: Toward Clarifying Some Fundamental Concepts of the Exercises" in *Ignatius of Loyola: His Personality and Spiritual Heritage, 1556–1956*, ed. by Friedrich Wulf (St. Louis: Institute of Jesuit Sources, 1977), pp. 200–236, esp. pp. 222–30.

49. Paul Robb, "Conversion as a Human Experience," *Studies in the Spirituality of Jesuits*, 14, no. 3 (1982), pp. 11–12.

50. *Ibid.*, pp. 21–22.

51. "It belongs to God alone to give consolation to the soul without previous cause, for it belongs to the Creator to enter into the soul, to leave it, and to act upon it, drawing it wholly to the love of His Divine Majesty. I say without previous cause, that is, without any previous perception or knowledge of any object from which such consolation might come to the soul through its own acts of intellect and will." *Spiritual Exercises*, p. 133.

52. "The Ignatian Process for Discovering the Will of God in an Existential Situation: Some Theological Problems in the Rules for Election and Discernment of Spirits in St. Ignatius' *Spiritual Exercises*" in *Ignatius of Loyola: His Personality and Spiritual Heritage, 1556–1956*, pp. 280–89; see also "Comments by Karl Rahner on Questions Raised by Avery Dulles," *ibid.*, pp. 290–93.

53. Rahner, "The Ignatian Process," p. 288.

54. "Comments," p. 292.

55. "First Conference of Abbot Moses," c. 20, *Nicene and Post-Nicene Fathers*, 2nd series, Vol. 11 (repr. Grand Rapids: Eerdmans, 1973), p. 304. "Make yourselves into prudent money-changers" is an agraphon, a statement attributed to Christ but not found in the canonical Gospels. See Hugo Rahner, *Ignatius the Theologian*, trans. by Michael Barry (New York: Herder and Herder, 1968), pp. 32–52.

56. See Joseph T. Lienhard, "On 'Discernment of Spirits' in the Early Church," *Theological Studies*, 41 (1980), 505–29 which traces the history of the understanding of the phrase "discernment of spirits" in the patristic period and provides valuable bibliographic references.

57. *The Life of Antony and the Letter to Marcellinus*, trans. by Robert C. Gregg (New York: Paulist Press, 1980), 22, pp. 47–48.

58. Cassian, p. 308.

59. John H. Wright, *A Theology of Christian Prayer* (New York: Pueblo, 1979), p. 135.

60. (New York: Simon and Schuster, 1978), pp. 271–84.

61. See William C. Spohn, "The Reasoning Heart: An American Approach to Christian Discernment," *Theological Studies*, 44 (1983), 30–52; and James M. Gustafson, "Moral Discernment in the Christian Life," in *Norm and Context in Christian Ethics*, ed. by Gene Outka and Paul Ramsey (New York: Scribners, 1968), pp. 17–36.

62. "Spiritual Discernment in *The Dialogue* of Saint Catherine of Siena," *Horizons*, 9 (1982), 48.

63. *Ibid.*, p. 49.

CHAPTER FOUR

Images and Stories
at Midlife

Conversion and discernment at midlife lead people to pay close attention to their own hearts. The heart is often the locus of conversion in the Scriptures, for it is in the heart that God can be found.[1] Ezechiel puts it succinctly in God's own expression: "A new heart I will give you, and a new spirit I will put within you; and I will take out of your flesh the heart of stone and give you a heart of flesh" (36:26). The heart is the source of feelings, imaginings, and desires, both the good and the bad. To talk of the human heart is to talk of roots.

At midlife the call to conversion is a call to examine the inner workings of the heart, to pay attention to what goes on in the interior of a person. But it is no easy task to notice the feelings, images, memories, desires, and thoughts which move within the human spirit. In fact, to enter into one's own depths and to take notice of what transpires there can be a frightening, dangerous enterprise. People often need the support of a concerned individual and the vision of a faith community to do this. Spiritual direction is intended to provide just this kind of support and vision.

Contemplation at Midlife

To pay attention to what is present in one's heart is to begin to contemplate. It is the road which leads to the discovery of one's true identity. Contemplation is a way of seeing reality in depth and it is related to discernment inasmuch as it focuses attention on what is really there either to be affirmed or rejected. Contemplation clears the path for further conversion because it allows people to experience their true condition. By paying attention to what is going on inside themselves, people discover images of themselves which are operative in their daily lives below the threshhold of their ordinary awareness. Some of these images need to be supported; others need to be overcome. Contemplation enables people to discover an image of themselves as rooted in God.

The way of contemplation is traditionally the way of personal reformation. In St. Paul's thought, people were to be reformed in the image of God in which they were created. "And we all, with unveiled face, beholding the glory of the Lord, are being changed into his likeness from one degree of glory to another; for this comes from the Lord who is the Spirit" (2 Cor 3:18). In the patristic period various metaphors for reclaiming the image of God were introduced. Origen (c.185–c.254) and Gregory of Nyssa (c.330–c.395) spoke of a mirroring of God in the human soul. Gregory of Nyssa also draws an analogy between the Gospel parable of the Lost Coin and the image of God in the human person. This image, Gregory suggests, is not really lost but hidden by a person's sin and uncleanness.[2]

Walter Hilton in the fourteenth century continued this same line of thought:

> "Cast out all . . . sins from your heart, sweep your soul clean with the broom of the fear of God, wash it with your tears, and you shall find your coin, Jesus. . . . He is within you, although he is lost to you; but you are not in him until you have found him. In this, too, is his mercy, that he would suffer himself to be lost only where he may be found. There is no need to travel to Rome or Jerusalem to search for him: but turn your thoughts into your own soul where he is hidden, and seek him there."[3]

Hilton speaks of a twofold reformation process leading to the highest contemplation. There is, first of all, a reformation in faith which requires efforts at overcoming sin. This is followed by a reformation in feeling wherein a new knowledge of God is given. The prerequisite for these reform movements is again deep self-knowledge. "Your soul is a spiritual mirror in which you may see the likeness of God. First, then, find your mirror, and keep it bright and clean from the corruption of the flesh and worldly vanity. In this life all chosen souls direct their effort and intention to this end although they may not be fully conscious of it."[4]

This process of discovering the deeper self correlates well with the movement toward interiority which is typical of midlife development. Jung valued religious traditions precisely because they fostered this voyage of self-discovery and provided means for staying in touch with the unconscious dimensions of the self. Jung suggested that focusing on the self as the image of God facilitated integration. "The spontaneous symbols of the self, or of wholeness, cannot in practice be distinguished from a God-image. . . . There is an ever-present archetype of wholeness which may easily disappear from the purview of consciousness or may never be perceived at all until a consciousness illuminated by conversion recognizes it in the figure of Christ. As a result of this *'anamnesis'* the original state of oneness with the God-image is restored. It brings about an integration, a bridging of the split in the personality caused by the instincts striving apart in different and mutually contradictory directions."[5]

To encourage people at midlife to pay close attention to what goes on inside them should not foster a sterile introspection. Rather, it should lead to an unveiling of the truth of the self and so to a humility which springs from an accurate perception of reality. It is not only the self which comes to be viewed differently but the world as well. The contemplative as seer penetrates beyond surface appearances. The Jesuit poet Gerard Manley Hopkins described this type of seeing when he spoke of perceiving the "inscape" rather than the "landscape." The inscape for Hopkins is a convergence (a 'tacit knowing' pointing toward God), a coming together of the phenomena of our experience into a unity of their source."[6]

Contemplation reveals what is really in the heart as well as in the surrounding world. It is a refined seeing which makes use of the imagination to uncover the hidden beauty of reality as wrought by God's hand. Thomas Merton in an essay on the contemplative life underlined the importance of imagination. "The imagination," Merton wrote, "is a discovering faculty, a faculty for seeing relationships, for seeing meanings that are special and even quite new. The imagination is something which enables us to discover unique present meaning in a given moment of our life. Without imagination the contemplative life can be extremely dull and fruitless."[7]

People at midlife can benefit by paying attention to the working of imagination in their lives. This faculty is sometimes neglected because it is thought unimportant in shaping a future and moving toward a closer relationship with God and with others. Yet the crucial role of imagination in a well integrated life is increasingly recognized by both mental health professionals and spiritual directors. Humanity made in the image of God can not afford to neglect the many other images which become operative in people's minds and either distort or reflect the goodness of the Creator.

Imagination and Midlife Development

At midlife the dream which has animated a person's life thus far is often called into question. Certain aspects of the dream may no longer be realizable. In some instances, when disillusionment sets in, the imagination runs dry and an imaginative shock is needed to get it into operation once again.[8] Such a shock comes when the pattern for one's life confronts a potential which far exceeds what that pattern has allowed thus far. In other words, the death of a dream does not foreshadow a life in which little can be accomplished. In fact, midlife can find the imagination pointing out new and exciting possibilities for the future precisely because they may be in a direction which was previously unthought of.

The rich man who so earnestly asked Jesus a question about salvation was ultimately paralyzed because of his own poverty of imagination. He could not imagine any future beyond the pattern he had so closely adhered to for so long. The parables of Jesus were intended to bring about the imaginative shock that would lead to new imaginings. In spiritual direction the role of the director is to stimulate the imagination of those who come for direction, to provide new perspectives, and to present the givens of one's life in a different light. For imagination is "the sum of all the resources within us that we employ to form accurate images of the self and its world. The imagination is concerned with the discovery of potentiality and new possibilities, with what is not yet, but only because it is oriented first of all toward actuality."[9]

As we have mentioned above, midlife brings an experience of limits when one's unbounded desire comes face-to-face with one's limited possibilities for achievement. Since the dream of youth may have to be given up and mourned at midlife, what is needed is not an escape into fantasy in order to console a wounded self but a renewed imagination which builds on accurate perceptions of the self and the world. Unlike fantasy which distorts reality in order to satisfy autistic needs, imagination is a gateway to a deeper contact with reality. Paying attention to fantasies can reveal some hidden wishes or unexpressed feelings, but cultivating the imagination can uncover a transcendent dimension in experience which can give new meaning to life.

Unfortunately many people discount imagination by appealing to "science" which purportedly functions according to the dictates of empirical method and pure logic. These same people, however, overlook the absolutely essential workings of imagination in the formulation of scientific theories and technological advances. Indeed, religious beliefs are sometimes regarded as the product of an overactive imagination and nothing more than dabbling in illusion. And yet illusion, which Freud used to categorize religious beliefs, is also recognized by him as not necessarily false, "unrealizable or in contradiction to reality."[10] Illusion, which springs from the imagination, can in fact penetrate below the surface of reality and apprehend the "more" that is present there.

"Illusion," comments the Jesuit analyst Meissner, "retains its ties to reality but also retains the capacity to transform reality into something that is permeated with meaning and inner significance. Man cannot do without illusion since it is that which gives meaning and sustenance to his experience of himself."[11] To employ illusion, then, is not to turn one's back on reality but rather to see through the holes in external reality. The poet does this when he or she captures in language an experience of the transcendent hidden in ordinary events. When one deals with illusion and its source, the creative imagination, one enters into a special way of seeing the profound meaning of experience. That is just the opposite of merely looking at surface appearances.

People at midlife are called to become artists, to discover the "more" within themselves and the world, and to share their discovery with others through the limited medium of their human lives. What can revitalize these people for this task is the capacity to take hold of an illusion or a vision of themselves in relation to the transcendent. The poet and essayist Ralph Waldo Emerson found such a vision in the encounter with nature. "How easily we might walk onward into the opening landscape, absorbed by new pictures and by thoughts fast succeeding each other, until by degrees the recollection of home was crowded out of mind, all memory obliterated by the tyranny of the present, and we were led in triumph by nature. . . . These enchantments are medicinal, they sober and heal us. These are plain pleasures, kindly and native to us."[13]

The ability to perceive something other than mere external phenomena is a special feature of a religious approach to reality. Rudolf Otto (1869–1937) in his classic *The Idea of the Holy* (*Das Heilige*, 1917) wrote of a faculty of divination, a talent for discerning the presence of the holy. He relates this talent to the earlier observation of Friedrich Schleiermacher (1768–1834) on intuitions of the sacred. "What Schleiermacher is feeling after is really the faculty or capacity of deeply absorbed *contemplation*, when confronted by the vast, living totality and reality of things as it is in nature and history. Whenever a mind is exposed in a spirit of absorbed submission to impressions of 'the universe,' it becomes capable—so he lays it down—of experiencing 'intuitions' and 'feelings' of something that is, as it were, a sheer overplus, in addition to empirical reality. . . [The import of these intuitions] is the glimpse of an Eternal, in and beyond the temporal and penetrating it, the apprehension of a ground and meaning of things in and beyond the empirical and transcending it. They are *surmises* or *inklings* of a Reality fraught with mystery and momentousness."[14]

This talent for perceiving the sacred is a facet of discernment. It is an exercise in faith and relies on the creative imagination for a true vision of reality. Conversion presupposes such an imaginative perception of a "more" in life which can lure people forward. Paul Ricoeur has suggested that conversion "which means much more than making a new choice . . . implies a shift in the direction of the look, a reversal in the vision, in the imagination, in the heart, before all kinds of good intentions and all kinds of good decisions and good actions."[15] Ricoeur also notes the role which parables can play in the conversion process. "To listen to the Parables of Jesus, it seems to me, is to let one's imagination be opened to the new possibilities disclosed by the extravagance of these short dramas. If we look at the Parables as at a word addressed first to our imagination rather than to our will, we shall not be tempted to reduce them to mere didactic devices, to moralizing allegories. We will let their poetic power display itself within us."[16]

Spiritual direction at midlife is an opportunity to reclaim dormant or worn-out imaginative abilities. Attention to the workings of the imagination can be a stepping stone to a renewed sense of purpose in life and a discovery of deeper meaning. The guiding illusion which has provided meaning so far in one's life can also be tested and reshaped. Paul Pruyser has spoken of "illusion-processing" as an ongoing part of religious development.[17] To process an illusion is to eliminate idiosyncratic distortions from a vision of transcendent reality. Direction is just such an exercise in illusion-processing. Such an exercise can have special relevance at midlife because of the effort a person must make to come to terms with the self and to deal with the narcissistic distortions of one's vision of life.

Recent developments in psychoanalytic object relations theory have shed light on the beginnings of illusion formation. Studies on the imagination in this psychoanalytic field can provide a helpful framework for understanding direction as a processing of people's images and illusions. D. W. Winnicott, a British pediatrician and psychoanalyst, noted the close attachment which older infants form to some special object, such as a blanket, a stuffed animal, or a toy.[18] The object, which Winnicott calls a transitional object, provides the child with soothing and comfort. It facilitates a child's adjustment to his or her growing awareness of separateness from mother, and it facilitates the child's gradual distinction of a subjective *inner* world of fantasy and feeling from *outer* reality. The transitional object is, according to Winnicott, the child's first "not-me possession"; it is part of the first attempt to establish a relationship to a world beyond the mother.

Yet the transitional object is a blend of the two worlds which the infant is trying to sort out. While it is a physical object and so a part of the external world, it is also invested with special significance from the child's own inner world. It becomes a mother-substitute because of a creative act by the infant who gives it a surplus meaning. This is the beginning of illusion formation. Winnicott notes how this activity of the infant is supported and shared by the rest of the family. Family members regard the object as special, even sacred, and handle it with reverence, and so the meaning of the transitional object is shared by them. Here are the humble beginnings of people's use of symbols. In religious traditions symbols come to have carefully articulated shared meanings.

Winnicott sees the infant's special object as a forerunner of a multitude of transitional phenomena which are embodied in culture, creative endeavors, and religion. Following this insight, one commentator on the poetry of Gerard Manley Hopkins claims: "[Hopkins] is not operating in the realm of what is objectively perceived; neither is he completely subjective. In fact, he seems to be in that transitional area between inner and outer which Winnicott found in young children. . . ,"[19] Winnicott himself argues: "I am here staking a claim for an intermediate state between a baby's inability and his growing ability to recognize and accept reality. I am therefore studying the substance of *illusion*, that which is allowed to the infant, and which in adult life is inherent in art and religion, and yet becomes the hallmark of madness when an adult puts too powerful a claim on the credulity of others, forcing them to acknowledge a sharing of illusion that is not their own. We can share a respect for *illusory experience*, and if we wish we may collect together and form a group on the basis of the similarity of our illusory experiences. This is a natural root of grouping among human beings."[20]

Paul Pruyser, pushing the formulations of Winnicott still further, has suggested that psychology has unduly limited the possibilities for human growth and development by focusing on a two-world vision—an inner world of autistic fantasy and an outer world of objective reality. Human development has traditionally been understood to involve curbing the urgings of fantasy in response to the demands of reality. Pruyser maintains we need to give place to a third world, an illusionistic world, which is the world of play and imagination. Meissner comes to a similar conclusion: "The need for a capacity for illusion, however it may be modified or diminished in the growth of objectivity and realistic adaptation, is never completely eliminated. In fact, in the healthy resolution of crises of development, there emerges a residual capacity for illusion which serves as one of the most important and significant dimensions of man's existence."[21]

The illusionistic world is the place where one encounters a sense of mystery. The objects found there are more than mere images produced by the individual mind and more than perceptual images produced as a result of the real world impinging upon the senses. As Pruyser elaborates: "Illusion also includes mystery: since it is beyond the merely subjective and the merely objective, it has a special object relationship endowed with many surplus values about whose legitimacy one does not bicker. Its validation lies in the encounter with the special object itself. And illusion also includes the holy: the special object is held as something sacred and so regarded by third parties also."[22]

That which comprises the illusionistic world is a great concern of spiritual direction. When one's personal illusion is threatened by distortions, when it is pulled out of the realm of a shared vision into private fantasy, or when it is distorted by being too closely identified with some external reality, direction tries to help the person to become aware of these distortions and correct them. In the best of situations both director and directee will share the illusion about life and reality which is enshrined in Christian beliefs. This interaction is in part what is meant by direction as illusion processing. At midlife various distortions can be responsible for experiences of boredom and frustration in the life of faith. Indeed a crisis of faith at midlife may be connected to some breakdown in illusionistic or transitional relatedness. "To recapture a sense of mystery and transcendence, people must be called back from 'thingish' and factual thought to imaginative thought, in which novelty of insight can be produced."[23]

To live in the illusionistic world is to be attuned to a particular type of relatedness. Patterns of relating to objects—persons, things, and the self—set up early in life can evolve to more mature levels as life goes on. Object relations theory within psychoanalysis is an attempt to describe this evolution. Relationships to a transcendent object bear the imprint of early patterns but they can also evolve. The relationship a person has to God is perhaps the best example, and we will discuss this at greater length in a following section. Directors can be of great assistance by enabling people to understand this relationship and by helping them to improve it. There is a considerable difference between the infant in relationship to some special object and the adult in relationship to a work of art, even though both have to do with the illusionistic world. Likewise, the relationship to God can develop throughout the course of a person's life.

To invite people at midlife into a closer engagement with the illusionistic world is to lead them into the sphere of creativity where they can do adventurous thinking and make inspired connections, going beyond both matter-of-fact reality and undisciplined fantasizing. In direction such thinking and connections can be shared and tested consensually to determine that they are not utterly fantastic or unresponsive to the potentialities that are present in a person's life. Symbols and ideals which challenge people to become something more than they have been so far can be examined with another person as a sounding board. "The realistic sphere," Pruyser observes, "in which we dwell with an attitude of 'that's the way things are' is always badly in need of infusions from the illusionistic sphere, which alone is capable of creating the ideals that may and should improve the conditions under which we live."[24]

So it is that people at midlife often find themselves in a situation analogous to that of the person at the beginning of the creative process. There is in both cases an initial experience of dissatisfaction with present reality. The creative person can focus on some puzzling aspect of a situation and see a critical issue begging for resolution. He or she is led to search for a new illusion, an inspiration, an imaginative way of solving the puzzle, of putting the pieces together in a new configuration. The creativity is a result of working with imagery and channeling energy in the direction of some transcendent reality.[25] Likewise, midlife, in Daniel Levinson's terms, requires a reworking, this time a reworking of the *life* structure. Spiritual direction seeks to foster a creative reworking of the life structure and orders it to the transcendent, shared ideals implicit in Christian beliefs.

The puzzles of midlife which call forth the powers of the imagination typically center on a self caught in a web of circumstance which seems to forestall any deep satisfaction. Ideals seem to be defective, and they hold a person captive with no apparent exit. For some, spiritual life itself seems to hold no promise and God even appears to have withdrawn to the peripheries of life, since anger and disappointment cloud their efforts to relate to a God who no longer soothes and comforts. The illusion of a God who rewards and the illusion of a life with transcendent meaning often seem like delusions. With puzzles such as these people often enter spiritual direction. There the breakdown of religious illusions calls for a deeper look at and a reassessment of a person's images of self and God. Distortions need to be removed, and the tendency to form defective images and ideals needs to be understood. The director helps a person to interpret the present impasse, stimulates the imagination, and assists in the discernment and formation of a new vision for life.

Images of Self at Midlife

This book has repeatedly pointed out the call which people at midlife experience to a deeper conversion. It has also focused upon the response to this call, which requires the exercise of discernment and all the related judgments which that implies. Entering into the realm of illusion and of imagination, where fuller meaning and renewed energy are found, midlife conversion leads a person to a clearer identity and to a more complete understanding of who they are both for themselves and for others. Thus, direction at midlife provides an opportunity for a person to assess the image of self upon which their sense of identity is based. Likewise, the image of one's ideal self, the person one would like to be, can also be examined.

The establishment of personal identity is not a task that is completed with adolescence. It is an ongoing process. In identity formation and *re*formation throughout a person's life, both positive and negative self-images are integrated to form an image of a unified "I" which is autonomous and yet which draws together and interrelates multiple images of the self.[26] As Erikson has described it for adolescence: "A pervasive sense of identity brings into gradual accord the variety of changing self-images which have been experienced during childhood (and which, during adolescence, are often recapitulated) and the role opportunities offering themselves to young persons for selection and commitment." He further notes, "a lasting sense of self cannot exist without a continuous experience of a conscious 'I' which is the numinous center of existence: a kind of *existential identity*, then, which sooner or later transcends the psychosocial one."[27]

At midlife people can firmly establish their sense of psychosocial identity on a broader base, and they can also get in closer touch with the numinous center of themselves of which Erikson speaks. This is to suggest that images of the self should be reviewed, although any given "I" is ultimately more than the images which lead to a sense of a continuous self. In direction the quest for true spiritual identity is a major goal. In this search people become aware of the interior battle of images of the self.[28] Although people may not be consciously aware of many of the negative and positive images, these images reveal themselves indirectly in feeling states and attitudes toward self and others.

Negative and inadequate images of the self are not changed by intellectual arguments but by the cultivation of more adequate images. People can challenge the negative images which surface in their lives and, more crucially, they can replace them with images more reflective of their deep value as persons made in the image of God. Both negative and positive images of oneself often have roots in the long history of relationships with significant others which is the breeding ground for a sense of self. Based on earlier relationships, a person may form an image of himself or herself as a victim—for example, a person whom others take unfair advantage of. Such an image then serves as an organizing frame for new and diverse experiences.[29] It can impede the formation of new relationships or the deepening of existing ones; even a person's relationship with God can be affected and brought to an impasse.

Because these images are often below the threshold of conscious awareness, personal effort is required to uncover them. A sensitive director can help people discover these images by drawing attention to feelings and impasses and wondering with them what image of self might be connected with the current situation. A director may also suggest some possible images which seem to be at work. In this activity the director is making hermeneutical judgments, interpreting phenomena in order to help a person arrive at the meaning of a situation. At times this will involve both director and directee in an archeological search for images rooted in a past not yet fully understood and appropriated.[30] These images will continue to hold sway until they are challenged and found inappropriate to the new situation and then replaced by more adequate images. Roger Gould, as we discussed earlier, describes the process of transformation precisely as a struggle to expand the boundaries of a self-definition by challenging childhood senses of the self and moving beyond them.

Personal prayer can be an occasion for people to come into contact with some of the negative images which pull them away from their true spiritual identity. Since sharing what happens in prayer is typically an important part of the direction process, direction provides a special opportunity for discussing the specifics of these negative images. Although these negative images may be dismissed as simply distractions unworthy of attention, taking note of them can provide insight into the shadow side of the self. These so-called distractions may serve as windows on one's envious and rivalrous feelings. Distractions can reveal the false self, those deviations from the full self which God intends a person to realize.[31]

Prayer is one clear way people can come to see themselves as divided selves in need of healing. "Instead of feeling besieged by autonomous forces of envy and hate, bad as they may be, the praying person experiences them as a rupturing of relationship to God and to his or her own deepest self. It is less a generalized 'evil' at this point and more a sense of 'sin,' a horrified awareness of one's own perjury against truth where truth has shown itself in the most personal of terms."[32] Such an experience often leads to confession which is not only the acknowledgment of one's own fault but also the recognition of God's mercy. The awareness of one's own sinful tendencies and one's constant need for God's mercy, furthermore, is a strong deterrent to the narcissistic distortion of the self as already fully converted. In this process directors help people to cultivate an image of themselves as forgiven, not just once, but time and time again.

So-called "distractions" in prayer can also reveal neglected potential within a person. The quest for truth demands attention to what is good in a person but also to what is neglected and undeveloped. Direction is a place where the fear which prevents a person from tapping such potential can be discussed. New images of the self are allowed to emerge which incorporate a revised understanding of the self and which help to mitigate the fear. Since midlife is a time for balancing polarities within the personality, images which give proper place to the neglected side, for instance, the masculine or the feminine, separateness or attachment, creativity or destruction, young or old, are especially relevant.

Ideals—those patterns for what people know they should become—can also surface in the context of prayer. The self is usually evaluated in terms of how it measures up to these ideal images; hence their great power. Yet ideals, like other parts of the illusionistic world, can be distorted. They can be fantastic visions more related to people's grandiose estimations of self or to their unfounded hopes than to an awareness of what is humanly possible. What is imagined as a goal for the self must come under the guidance of a critical reasoning process which takes accurate account of human limitations.

In direction people are helped to distinguish between autistic fantasy and the creative imagination which builds on facts and clear perceptions of reality. William Lynch speaks of life as a "broken but steady movement out of the omnipotent self-image of the child into the finite but real self-image of the adult. . . . The important thing is the discovery that this is a stronger and more effective, a more powerful way, rather than a weaker one. For reality and limitation are charged with power, whereas the child is not. . . . When we give up omnipotence we only give up fantasy. We give up only false hopes which, when frustrated, as they must be, produce only anger or despair."[33]

Midlife entails coming to terms with remnants of childhood omnipotence. Unrealistic expectations of life and self must be given up if this passage is to be successfully negotiated. In direction, a person's expectations with regard to the spiritual life and one's relationship to God need to be questioned; for these, too, can be fanciful. A story from the desert tradition of ancient monasticism illustrates this point: "Abbot Pastor said that Abbot John the Dwarf had prayed to the Lord and the Lord had taken away all his passions, so that he became impassible. And in this condition he went to one of the elders and said: You see before you a man who is completely at rest and has no more temptations. The elder said: Go and pray to the Lord to command some struggle to be stirred up in you, for the soul is matured only in battles. And when the temptations started up again he did not pray that the struggle be taken away from him, but only said: Lord, give me strength to get through the fight."[34]

Letting go of certain images of self, defective ideals, and unrealistic expectations constitute losses for people at any age. At midlife the sense of loss may be especially great because so much energy has been spent in the first part of life in the service of these ideals and images. Mourning is a typical and necessary reaction to these losses. There is a sadness and certain feelings of depression as the attachment to these things is given up.[35] Directors can suggest that this is simply a part of the dying and rising which Christians must undergo in the experience of conversion. They can direct people's attention to the rewards which come from meeting more reasonable goals and from discovering a deeper sense of identity in new self-images.

Interpretation and Spritual Identity

Personal history is the raw material which the imagination works upon as it processes images. The disciplined imagination judiciously selects and shapes images gathered from experience, and out of them it creates an identity for the self. To establish one's identity is to interpret one's own personal history; it is a process of consciously and unconsciously selecting out certain experiences and related images as central. Identity represents only a partial understanding of personal history, and it does not exhaust the possibilities for identity formation inherent in that history.[36] Thus, imagination is not opposed to reason, but it can make use of reasoning abilities to provide guidance in the establishment of a balanced self-identity. Imagination must be controlled and directed by reason or a person will regress into the autistic world of pure fantasy and move away from the world of shared values and illusion.

Identity formation is an ongoing process in the course of a person's life precisely because personal history is never fully understood, and it needs to be digested again and again. Memories surface in prayer, as well as dreams, and various other activities, and all these present new opportunities for deeper self-understanding. Because at midlife the tendency to defend against such memories by denial and repression is lessened, as Vaillant has noted, direction at midlife provides an excellent opportunity for reclaiming and reinterpreting past experiences.

To seek the truth about oneself is to appropriate one's own past history. At midlife a deeper understanding of one's childhood is not only possible but desirable. Present limitations, even enslavements, become more comprehensible when they are viewed in the light of early life experiences. But a review of the past can also foster greater freedom in the present. As one analyst has observed: "What is possible is to engage in the task of actively reorganizing, reworking, creatively transforming those early experiences which, painful as many of them have been, first gave meaning to our lives. The more we know what it is that we are working with, the better we are able to weave our history which, when all is said and done, is recreating, in ever-changing modes and transformations, our childhood. To be an adult means that; it does not mean leaving the child in us behind."[37]

Human development, rather than progressing in a straight line, is best imagined as an ascending spiral in which the themes a person dealt with early in life reappear. Memories of past experiences come to the surface when experiences of a similar nature are met in the present. They point up the unfinished quality of our human existence.

Interpretations of personal history, from which a sense of personal identity arises, are likewise best thought of as an ascending spiral. A person's identity is understood against the background of his or her personal history; this is where the explanation of a person's sense of self is found. There is a dialectical relationship here between the part (identity) and the whole (personal history). In interpretation theory the term *hermeneutic circle* describes this movement back and forth between part and whole, understanding and explanation, identity and personal history.[38] Identity finds its validation in the personal history which it seeks to interpret.

New interpretations or new senses of identity arise as people enter again and again into their own personal histories through ongoing memorial activity. In the dialogue of the direction relationship, new meanings are discovered as a person talks about his or her personal history to a director. One circle of meaning is replaced by another which builds upon but goes beyond the previous one. Analogous to the developmental spiral, there is a "hermeneutical spiral"; with age and additional experience there is added reflection and new understandings of personal history.[39] What starts a movement to a new level of interpretation is the imaginative shock mentioned above, the trauma of discovering the disparity between life as it has been lived and the potential which remains untapped. Personal history is then interpreted not as a justification for a current state of affairs but as pointing in a new direction transcending previous expectations. Research on midlife suggests the possibility of just such a change in interpretation.

Peter Homans has suggested that there is a correlation between developmental stages and hermeneutical styles or modes of interpretation.[40] Like Fowler's developmental stages of faith, Homans describes a progression in later stages to a renewed appreciation of symbols. Fowler spoke of a conjunctive faith as typically emerging at midlife, a faith which attempts to draw together rational understanding and symbols to express a dimension of depth in life and in the self. Homans notes that what happens in interpretation is an awakening to "prospective symbols," a term used by Ricoeur for that level of symbolization where traditional symbols are seen as vehicles of new meanings. Rather than a person interpreting the meaning of life simply in terms of the past, he or she constructively reinterprets, opening the past to new possibilities for the future.[41]

Symbols and Master Images

Self-images are symbols in their own right inasmuch as they possess multiple meanings.[42] Ricoeur writes of symbols as having a literal meaning which points to a deeper and inexhaustible meaning.[43] Thus standard self-images can be explored for new meanings. They have a density to them which is not exhausted in any one interpretation. Likewise the impact of religious symbols on self-images can suggest new perspectives of the self. People at midlife come to direction with the hope of gaining a religious perspective on their struggles. The symbols which the Church offers in its creedal statements and ritual performances as well as in the Scriptures are vehicles for self-understanding.

Exposing oneself to the symbols which the Church offers opens a person to a new sense of identity. Though the appropriation of religious symbols for the purpose of self-understanding is a life-long task, David Burrell has noted how at midlife people discover a new sense to their being "sinners." That is only one among many symbols which the Church offers.[44] Midlife brings an awareness of sin as found in tendencies rooted deep in the human heart rather than in specific misdeeds. Typically people at midlife come to see their relentless drive for success and for making something of themselves as an aspect of the demonic or destructive in themselves. Such symbols and symbolic expressions provide a context for growth into the full humanity symbolized in Jesus Christ.

The human person as an image of God is still another symbolic expression which the Church offers for people's self-understanding. The Scriptures abound in other positive images for the self, which directors can ask people to focus their prayer upon. Inadequate or evil images are also presented in the Scriptures, and these serve as reminders of the struggle which people face in the realm of imagination and fantasy. The Church is a supportive community where such images can be faced and overcome. The direction relationship is one facet of this support, and it complements the larger series of nurturing and challenging relationships found within the Church.[45]

Most importantly the Church presents the person of Jesus Christ as a key image for understanding the self and reality. It presents the revelation accomplished in Christ which has disclosed the true nature of the world. "Jesus Christ is the symbolic form with which the self understands itself, with the aid of which it guides and forms itself in its actions and its sufferings."[46] Carl Jung saw the importance of Christ as a symbol in the quest for wholeness which is so prominent at midlife. "Looked at from the psychological standpoint, Christ, as the Original Man . . . represents a totality which surpasses and includes the ordinary man, and which corresponds to the total personality that transcends consciousness. We have called this personality the 'self'."[47] Jung's statement approaches the description of the transcendent goal of humanity described in Ephesians 4: 13—"until we all attain to the unity of the faith and of the knowledge of the Son of God, to mature manhood, to the measure of the stature of the fulness of Christ."

Jung saw the events in the life of Christ as paradigmatic for the process of self-realization. "The drama of the archetypal life of Christ describes in symbolic images the events in the conscious life—as well as in the life that transcends consciousness—of a man who has been transformed by his higher destiny."[48] According to Jung's theory, symbols affected all the faculties of a person. "As a uniter of opposites, the symbol is a totality which can never be addressed only to one faculty in a man—his reason or intellect, for example—but always concerns our wholeness, touches and produces a resonance in all four of our functions at once. The symbol as 'image' has the character of a summons and stimulates a man's whole being to a total reaction; his thought and feeling, his senses and his intuition participate in this reaction and it is not, as some mistakenly suppose, a single one of his functions that is actualized."[49]

Religious symbols help to draw order out of the chaos people may experience at midlife. They are powerful unifiers, drawing into a whole one's fragmented self and life. The midlife transition is a passage from an old way of ordering life, through a chaotic period when the old order breaks down, to a new order in which polarities are more adequately balanced and reconciled. Arnold van Gennep, an anthropologist, noted how transition rites traditionally supported such passages from one state to another.[50] The in-between state was a condition of liminality, a threshhold existence where an individual was neither in the old state nor yet in the new. Symbols were offered to make the experience of the "passenger" comprehensible. Rites of incorporation or initiation brought the period of transition to an end.

Christian rituals, such as the Eucharist, can speak effectively and energetically to the experience of midlife "passengers." Directors can, therefore, capitalize on people's involvement in ritual activity and sensitize them to the symbols as means of discovering a new depth in their experience and in themselves. Such symbols provide perspective in a confusing and sometimes incomprehensible passage. The cross and the paschal event can illuminate the dying and rising to self which midlife entails. There is an openness to symbols especially when one's established structures are left behind in the midlife quest for better structures. Ritual and symbols help a person to name this experience of chaos and channel energy into new ways of relating to the self and to the world.[51] "The existence of community rituals, which express common beliefs in common symbols and common disciplines, serves to assure the person-in-crisis that what he or she is going through is not only meaningful, but also good; and not only good, but necessary for the well-being both of themselves and of the whole community."[52]

The rituals and symbols of the Church help people at midlife to die to certain images of themselves which held sway during the first half of their lives. The confrontation with death in ritual symbols of dying and rising can be the occasion for individuals to let go of a self-image of being in control. In the face of eventual (and approaching) death, the midlife adult relinquishes the obsessive need to be master of his or her own destiny and moves toward a surrender to a power beyond. This surrender is realized in many different ways throughout the course of the second half of life. Jesus' words to Peter indicate the suffering that is entailed: "When you were young, you girded yourself and walked where you would; but when you are old, you will stretch out your hands, and another will gird you and carry you where you do not wish to go" (Jn 21:18).

In the East, Zen masters guide their disciples to a surrender of the controlling self through the practice of an art. Eugen Herrigel, a German philosopher who taught in Japan, has described his experience of learning Zen in the context of the art of archery. His Western mind struggled against the surrender which was required; he wanted to be in control, he wanted to shoot the arrow. He recalled, "One day I asked the Master: 'How can the shot be loosed if "I" do not do it?' ' "It" shoots,' he replied."[53] People at midlife struggle between an attitude of willingness and an obstinate attitude of willfulness. The latter is "the setting of oneself apart from the fundamental essence of life in an attempt to master, direct, control, or otherwise manipulate existence."[54] Willingness, on the other hand, has to do with seeing oneself as part of a larger process.

People can cultivate certain master images to help them in the process of self-surrender at midlife. Master images give perspective and enable a person to reconcile other more specific images of self. The "self as player" is one such master image; a person places the ultimate seriousness of life in God's hands. In other words, a person relativizes his or her labors in the light of what God is doing in the world. Consequently, he or she can take the self less seriously and adopt a playful attitude toward life. This prevents idolatry of the self and allows for a growing trust in a God who will bring all things to a successful conclusion. At the same time, he or she knows that life is to be lived according to the norms of justice and fairness. If life is viewed as a game, it is, nevertheless, a game that requires fairness and sincere efforts to do one's part.[55]

Spiritual directors perform a great service when they assist people in the light of faith to take themselves less seriously. The human quest for acceptance is put in perspective when one is reminded that he or she has already been definitively accepted by God. Any previous drivenness can be effectively called into question. "God shows his love for us in that while we were yet sinners Christ died for us. Since, therefore, we are now justified by his blood, much more shall we be saved by him from the wrath of God. For if while we were enemies we were reconciled to God by the death of his Son, much more, now that we are reconciled, shall we be saved by his life" (Rom 5: 8–10).

Another helpful master-image at midlife is the self as sufferer: each person is acted upon by the attitudes and actions of others. In other words, no one has a perfectly free space in which to realize him or herself. Everyone experiences certain restrictions due to outside forces. Sometimes outside forces work toward the enrichment of possibilities for realization.[56]

A third master image which fits well with the whole process of spiritual direction is the self as responder. H. Richard Niebuhr treated this image in the context of Christian ethics: a person comes to understand the self as living in the presence of other selves and responding to this action upon him or herself. This implies for the Christian a task of interpretation whereby he or she comes to see the actions of others as conveying God's own action. With regard to Christ as a paradigm of responsibility Niebuhr says: "He interprets all actions upon him as signs of the divine action of creation, government, and salvation and so responds to them as to respond to divine action."[57] In the light of this self-image, the believer asks him or herself how God's larger action in the world touches his or her life. This transforms narcissism into areas of concern beyond selfish interests and preoccupations. Meaning for the self is found within a universal frame of reference which extends even beyond one's own church community.[58]

Directors can very profitably focus people's attention on their images of self. They can also suggest images from the Scriptures which can generate new interpretations of current dilemmas and past history. Yet there remains a self which is beyond any images, the mysterious center of the human person which some people encounter at midlife. This mystery of the self, more than any other, mirrors the mystery of the Godhead. Processing images of self and the growing sense of the mystery of personhood often parallels the processing of images of God and the meeting of the God beyond images. Images of God are often closely correlated with images of self. Spiritual direction is a place where a person can look at both.

Images of God

In Willa Cather's novel, *The Professor's House*, the midlife protagonist, Professor St. Peter, struggles for knowledge about himself. He gradually sorts out his social self from a deeper level of self. "Because there was marriage, there were children. Because there were children, and fervour in the blood and brain, books were born as well as daughters. His histories, he was convinced, had no more to do with his original ego than his daughters had; they were a result of the high pressure of young manhood."[59] At one point in his effort at self-understanding, he comes to appreciate the imaginative side of himself. "St. Peter had always laughed at people who talked about 'day-dreams,' just as he laughed at people who naively confessed that they had 'an imagination.' All his life his mind had behaved in a positive fashion. When he was not at work, or being actively amused, he went to sleep. He had no twilight stage. But now he enjoyed this half-awake loafing with his brain as if it were a new sense, arriving late, like wisdom teeth."[60]

His journey in self-exploration leads St. Peter to a discovery of the inner core of his being. Cather writes, "He seemed to be at the root of the matter; Desire under all desires, Truth under all truths. He seemed to know, among other things, that he was solitary and must always be so; he had never married, never been a father. He was earth, and would return to earth."[61] In the end St. Peter surrenders control over his destiny and opens himself to new possibilities in his life. Such a journey into the depths of oneself would open a religious person to a new vision of God which would correlate with an emerging sense of self.

Thomas Merton has noted the close interrelationship of the deeper self and God. "Finding our heart and recovering this awareness of our inmost identity implies the recognition that our external everyday self is to a great extent a mask and a fabrication. It is not our true self. And indeed our true self is not easy to find. It is hidden in obscurity and nothingness at the center where we are in direct dependence on God."[62] Discovering the truth of the self creates the situation where people discover the God within who sustains all life. This God can be approached through traditional images, new images, or in a way which transcends images.

Just as there is in human maturation a movement toward more adequate images of self and ultimately a movement beyond images to the mystery of the self, so there is in religious development a movement toward more adequate images of God and toward the God beyond all images. Images of God and images of self are often closely intertwined. Prayer is the place where these images can interact. People meet God as the one whom they imagine him to be, but these images of God evolve throughout the course of a person's life. Furthermore, changes in self-images are usually the occasion for corresponding revisions in God-images.[63]

Images of God are important ingredients in people's lives of faith. The sociologist Andrew Greeley has stated: "Tell me what your image is of God, your picture of Jesus, your fantasy of an afterlife, and I will know a good deal more about you religiously than if I just know how often you go to church or whether you believe in papal infallibility."[64] Images of God guide people's religious behavior and have a profound effect on their feeling states in private prayer, public worship, and everyday activity. As it is with images of self, different images of God often oppose one another in people's imaginations. For example, the image of God as stern judge can be played off against the image of God as merciful father.

Disappointed expectations, feelings of isolation and boredom, intense conflicts with one's sexual feelings and aggressiveness—all such midlife phenomena can lead a person to reconsider their relationship to God and the images they employ in dealing with God. Some people may consider God to be a source of their problems; others feel deserted by him at a crucial time of need; still others wonder whether belief in God is a facet of some larger refusal to grow up and live in the adult world. Directors may encounter people like this and many other people who simply sense a need to reconsider who God is in light of their own reconstructed sense of identity.

Although there is a host of traditional images of God, such as King, Father, Mother, Redeemer, and so on, each person arrives at what might be termed their own "core-image" on the basis of his or her own life experience. A person's image of God usually has very human origins, but it can supersede them. To discuss images of God is to enter once again the all important area of illusion. God-images like other illusionistic objects are composed of elements from an outer world combined with elements from subjective experience. The image of God, according to William Meissner, "is thus personalized and carries with it idiosyncratic elements corresponding to the individuality inherent in the believer's own sense of self—that is, the distinctive qualities and characteristics which distinguish him from all other men. . . . Each man [or woman] creates his [or her] own image of God, even though that personalized and individualized image is in contact with and in dialogue with a shared set of communal beliefs, which delineate the concept of God to which the group of believers pledges adherence."[65]

Research on the specific determinants of a person's God-image goes on. In a theory of God-imagery which deals only with males, Freud hypothesized that a young boy forms a God-image on the basis of his experience with his father: "A little boy is bound to love and admire his father who seems to him the most powerful, the kindest and the wisest creature in the world. God himself is after all only an exaltation of this picture of a father as he is represented in the mind of early childhood."[66] According to Freud's theory, when a young boy of five or six begins to identify with his father and sees him as a more human person, the old exalted image of his father is transformed into an image of God. The boy then has a God whom he can love and use as a protector and a source of love. Freud suggested that a later relationship to God varied in correspondence to the relationship to the natural father or other father figures. He did not see a place for the God-image in the life of a mature adult.[67]

Although contemporary research has gone considerably beyond Freud's conclusions, especially by incorporating the feminine dimension, his formulation contains valid elements. Hans Küng has observed: "Often enough a believer's image of God springs, not from original insight and free decision, but from an *image of a vindictive or kind father* imprinted at an early age. Often enough early childhood experiences with adults who appear as 'gods' are *transferred* both positively and negatively *to God*, so that behind the image of God the image of one's own father becomes visible, even though the latter has long been forgotten or repressed (it is the same with the mother image as reflected in the Mother of God or in Mother Church)."[68]

Midlife, which typically brings a sharpened awareness of one's own aging and the eventual, if not already realized, death of one's parents, pushes people to reexamine their views of God as Father. A paternalistic image of God sometimes sustains a sense of connectedness with one's natural father. At midlife many people may feel prompted to surrender the paternalistic image of God and to allow themselves to grow into a new way of relating to God. Dying to cherished images of God (as to cherished images of self) gives rise to a period of mourning. The psychiatrist Gerald May has written about his own feelings surrounding the giving up of a paternalistic image of God: "I am aware . . . that I clung to a paternalistic image of God for years after my own father died. I was nine at the time he passed away, and clinging to my old image of God provided me with some sense of ongoing relatedness to my father. When that paternalistic image of God finally died many years later, I re-experienced many of the feelings I had had concerning my father's death. Some of these were stronger with the passing of the God-image than they had been with my father's passing. In fact, my preconditioning to relate to God-as-father had helped me freeze my orientation to God."[69]

Recent research on God-imagery suggests that a person's experience with their mother as well as that with their father is significant in the formation of their first God-image. It also suggests that the image and the relationship to it is more dynamic and evolving than Freud allowed. This contemporary understanding of the formation of a God-image is based on object-relations theory which gives central place to early relationships to primary figures (parents, close relatives, others who live in the same house, etc.) in the constitution of the personality and the establishment of a relationship to the world. When the notion of God is first introduced to a child, usually in response to his or her questions about the cause of things, the child images this superior being as similar to his or her parents, only of greater power and size. The child fleshes out this notion of God on the basis of his or her previous interpersonal experience with parents and other significant figures. The God-image is a new and original creation of the child's which is created out of the "matrix of facts and fantasies, wishes, hopes and fears, in the exchange with those incredible beings called parents."[70]

The first God-image is reshaped at each stage of life. Ana-Maria Rizzuto has stated: "Those who are capable of mature religious belief renew their God representation to make it compatible with their emotional, conscious, and unconscious situation, as well as their cognitive and object-related development."[71] Yet for some people, the image of God does not get revised, and so it becomes unrelated to the current sense of self. That unrevised image can reflect and reinforce certain characteristics of parents which are contrary to one's growing sense of belief about the nature of God's relationship to people. For example, some people may at midlife still find themselves burdened with an image of God which is harsh and vengeful. While others may delight in communication with a God who is imaged as a loving source of comfort, one who challenges them to grow in love.

Direction can provide the opportunity for getting more closely in touch with one's core-image of God, an image which influences the way one relates to God personally. The feelings one has in prayer are clues to the underlying God-imagery in one's life. Prayer can also be the arena for reshaping this image and removing distortions which have blocked the development of a deeper God relationship.[72] The core-image is multifaceted and gives rise to many more specific images which color one's prayer and conversation about God. The appropriation of new specific images can help in the process of revising one's core-image. Theological reflection on the nature of God adds a dimension of richness to the image.

The use of a multiplicity of specific images for God can prevent the setting up of any one of them as an idol. Masculine and feminine images as well as personal and impersonal ones all point to the richness of the mystery of God. No one image nor even all of them together can express all of what God is for humanity. The images merely provide glimpses of the greater reality through the doorway of human experience and relatedness.[73] As a person matures, some images are discarded because they no longer speak to the heart about the reality of God. Repeated exposure to the Word of God (the Scriptures) helps transform the imagination and presents more adequate images of God. Parables suggest that God is beyond the images fashioned by one's wishes about what God should be. They call into question narcissistic distortions and reveal a God who exceeds human comprehension.[74]

In the normal process of religious development, people often become more aware of the God beyond images. As we have suggested, this movement beyond images correlates with a growing awareness of the mystery of the self. It also seems to correspond to a different type of religious experience.

Meissner describes three levels of religious experience which arise from three simultaneous lines of development in the human personality.[75] The first of these lines is the evolution throughout one's life from the infant's state of complete narcissism toward an identification with others and a love for them. The second line of development is the movement from a state of absolute dependence on others toward one of relative dependence and eventually relative independence. The third line is the development of faith itself away from an infantile sureness to a mature, discerning trust. The religious experience of an adult, analyzed in terms of these three lines, will reflect a particular attitude toward self, a greater or lesser degree of dependence, and a particular stage of faith development.

At midlife, as narcissism, dependence, and faith continue to evolve and undergo transformations, a person's God-images and their experienced relationship to God likewise evolve. As people struggle to gain a sense of integrity through accepting their successes and failures in life, Rizzuto suggests that the God image is questioned: Does it adequately represent the existing God? The God image which can emerge at this time is more attuned to the mystery of God. People at this point in their lives might express their belief in God by a formula such as "I accept you whatever you are." In describing their religious experience, they might say, "The ways of the Lord are mysterious."[76]

The recognition of the God beyond images often leads to a deeper relationship, but this recognition can be frightening at first. Thomas Merton observed: "Here we are advancing beyond the stage where God made himself accessible to our mind in simple and primitive images. We are entering the night in which he is present without any image, invisible, inscrutable, and beyond any satisfactory mental representation. . . . [A person's] prayer may become an obscure and hateful struggle to preserve the images and trappings which covered his [or her] emptiness. Either he [or she] will have to face the truth of his [or her] emptiness or else he [or she] will beat a retreat into the realm of images and analogies which no longer serve for a mature spiritual life."[77]

Directors can support people in their struggle with the darkness. Support is often a matter of declaring that faith can be deepened in the struggle. The God who is discovered in the darkness is the one who alone can meet the deep loneliness of the human heart. The analyst Harry Guntrip who addresses the issue of religion and personal integration concludes: "Religion is a way of experiencing the universe that does not condemn us all to a meaningless isolation *but* relates us to a personal heart of reality, that we refer to by the indefinable term 'God,' experienced but not explained, the 'ultimate indefinable mystery.' "[78]

New images which ground hope and support transcendence can emerge from the imagination once a person surrenders to the mystery of God. Images at one point are given up only to be reclaimed with the realization of their inadequacy and yet their indispensability for cherishing the experience of the sacred. In the lifelong processing of images of self and God, the Christian story of dying in order to rise is told again and again.

Life Story and Sacred Story

Both images of self and images of God become comprehensible in the framework of the stories which contextualize them and relate them to various experiences within people's lives. Spiritual direction is one place among many where storytelling goes on. It is by the stories people tell about themselves that both directors and the people themselves arrive at a fairly adequate sense of their identities. Stanley Hauerwas has underscored the value of stories:

> A story . . . is a narrative account that binds events and agents together in an intelligible pattern. We do not tell stories simply because they provide us a more colorful way to say what can be said in a different way, but because there is no other way we can articulate the richness of intentional activity—that is, behaviour that is purposeful but not necessary. For any good novelist knows there is always more involved in any human action than can be said. To tell a story often involves our attempt to make intelligible the muddle of things we have done in order to have a self.[79]

Human experience has an inherently narrative character. It is an incipient story, stored in memory as a temporal succession of moments. In an important study on narrative and experience, Stephen Crites has noted: "Storytelling is not an arbitrary imposition upon remembered experience, altogether alien to its own much simpler form. Images do not exist in memory as atomic units, like photographs in an album, but as transient episodes in an image-stream, cinematic, which I must suspend and from which I must abstract in order to isolate a particular image. The most direct and obvious way of recollecting it is by telling a story, though the story is never simply the tedious and unilluminating recital of the chronicle of memory itself."[80] As we discussed earlier in the section on identity, interpretation of one's personal history is involved in the process of identity formation. Likewise, storytelling involves an interpretation of the personal experiences which are found stored in a person's memory.

Storytelling is a process of retrieving and reworking the past which provides people with a solid footing in the present and helps them anticipate the future. To tell a story requires that a person find an imaginative ordering to his or her experience.[81] Storytelling has a central place in spiritual direction as well as in other helping processes. In reference to psychiatry, Bernice Neugarten has remarked: "The psychiatrist who uses any of the relational therapies helps the patient to create coherence and to make a meaningful life story from a life history. In doing so, both patient and therapist deal always with time and age and timing, whether it is a young patient who is relating a short past to a long future or an old patient who is relating a long past to a short future."[82]

Spiritual direction at midlife can be the occasion for digesting the past so that it becomes a resource in the present.[83] In listening to people's stories of their past, directors assist them in reintegrating past, present, and future into a coherent, meaningful story. Remembering is more than a simple recall of the past; it is a recollection in the sense of a re-collecting of memories into new configurations produced by thought and imagination. The stories which spiritual directors hear are interpretations of an individual's past. The task of direction is often to facilitate a "restorying" of life in order to make better sense of the past and open it more fully to the future.[84]

The spoken story can be approached as a text which has a deeper meaning than that which is immediately perceived by the speaker. Through the dialogue which is central to direction, layers of meaning in the text are exposed both to the director and to the storyteller. In the very telling the narrator learns something about him or herself that was not available before. Possible distortions in the text and misreadings of past situations are examined and opened up to new interpretations. Robert Steele has expressed the matter this way: "We have become distorted texts in need of interpretation and although we can never escape ourselves, we are capable of thought and reflection and so we can take up different analytic perspectives on ourselves."[85] Direction appeals to the imagination to find a new order hidden in the past.

Although the past should not be viewed reductively as the explanation for everything in the present, nevertheless the past can help people understand their present suffering. Injuries suffered in childhood which continue to constrict the exercise of freedom need to be reintegrated. Individuals who are still trying to please parents, who never took appropriate pleasure in the abilities of their children, need to rework their pasts. Present suffering with painful roots in life history needs to be accepted. It is healthy to mourn what was never provided in early life, for there can never be complete compensation. Painful personal history is often forgotten or denied, but the scars left on the psyche are all too real. In encouraging a person to accept his or her past history, direction also offers a new, redeeming perspective on it.[86]

For believers this process of accepting their personal histories can approximate "anamnesis," the ritual recollection of saving events which makes the power of those events present; for memories of God's past actions empower believers in their lives now.[87] Or, in other words, a person's past experiences of the graciousness of life provide reason for hope in moments of distress. As soon as an Other is remembered and recognized as having been present at various past stages in life, a person gains a new perspective at midlife. People can now discern that this mysterious Other whom they have encountered and to whom they have been asked to give some consent was God. John Dunne has written: "There is a task at each stage that begins with a consciousness and ends with a consent. The world emerges into consciousness, then sexuality, then mortality, and then spirit. . . . If one does succeed in consenting, then the thing that has emerged into consciousness becomes something human. It loses its divine and uncanny quality and becomes part of one's humanity. When that happens, one comes up against God. It is as though the Yes were a Yes to someone and not merely a Yes to something, a Yes to God and not merely a Yes to the world, to sexuality, to mortality, to spirit."[88]

At this juncture, many people discover that a sacred story *has* given shape and form to their own personal stories. It is, for example, a myth of creation which has guided their understanding of the transformation of chaos into a pattern of order in their own individual lives. Such myths or sacred stories "orient the life of people through time, their life-time, their individual and corporate experience and their sense of style, to the great powers that establish the reality of their world."[89] These sacred stories expressed in the Scriptures have had their effect. Christians believers come to deeper understanding of their own stories in the light of these. "The story of Jesus," William Spohn writes, "makes a normative claim upon Christian discern-

112

ment. It is not just any story, but one which claims our lives by asserting that it must be the truth of those lives. This is the story which reveals in a definitive way God's intentions for the world and for us."[90]

Christian spiritual direction at midlife can also be the context within which a correspondence of stories is realized. There are times when people's own stories are brought into direct confrontation with sacred story as articulated in the Scriptures and celebrated in the Christian community. This enables people to see more clearly the sacred dimensions of their own life stories and they can also make explicit connections (or contrasts) between their own life experiences and what has been described in revelation. Conversion is promoted by this exercise, because one's personal history can be reworked and reinterpreted in the light of the sacred story. As Edward King has remarked: "The story of the life, death, and resurrection of Jesus of Nazareth is retained not just as an extraordinary item of historical interest. It is retained as putting words in our mouths to diagnose, name and claim the accompaniment of God throughout life, death and resurrection in our experience."[91]

Interpretation is at issue here again. Some people have always interpreted the sacred story of God revealed in Jesus simply as God intervening from the outside on humanity's behalf. This intervention-ist interpretation of God's activity vis-a-vis humanity makes the world of human experience a closed system into which God periodically and dramatically inserts Himself. In this kind of system a man or woman just waits passively for God's coming. John Shea has related this type of interpretation to a certain way of imaging God. "Once the imagination pictures God as a supreme being over-against us, our sensitivities are geared for intervention. Unless God walks through the door, he is not there. The universal presence of God is overlooked while we scan the horizon for a particular intervention. This is not a question of either the existence [or] activity of God but a recognition of the limits of religious imagination."[92]

Another very different kind of interpretation does not focus on discreet activities of God in human history but on God's enduring intention for humanity. This intentional interpretation understands God as operating from *inside* human history not from the outside. Here God is imaged as a pervasive presence who is deeply involved in all of human life. In this interpretation Shea remarks: "The Cross is

113

God loving us from the inside. God has accepted those aspects of our lives we ourselves have disowned and denied. . . . This accepting presence of God goes beyond our carefully selective self-images. . . . God is redemptively present to every moment of human life and therefore even in our sin and suffering we are not abandoned."[93]

Midlife can be a time for discovering and appropriating this intentional interpretation of stories. This discovery can relate to a growing realization of how the Other for whom a person has searched has been present all along in the diverse experiences of life as a sustaining and supporting presence. In reviewing one's life history at midlife, a person can become more aware of God's presence in all their experiences. God is thus recognized as the base upon which all valuing and all meaning has been founded. This presence can be explicitly acknowledged; grace has been operative and now it impels to a deeper belief.[94]

Sacred stories themselves can invite this shift to an intentional interpretation, to this different understanding of God's involvement in human life. "When the parables and sayings of Jesus function as imaginative shock," Shea observes, "they result in the hearer's perceptual shift. . . . They do not change the content of thought but the framework with which one thinks."[95] This shift in framework or mode of interpretation is an important dimension of midlife conversion. The sacred stories can also engender a new discernment of God's presence in events which have been taken for granted or even dismissed as not a locus for God's presence and activity. Choices can now be deliberately made on the basis of what advances the story of a person's life in accord with the paradigm provided by the sacred stories. "To be truly responsible in faith, Christians need to imitate Jesus in seeking out the hidden divine intention by locating even destructive events in the context of God's creating, redeeming, and judging activity."[96]

Directors help people at midlife to create "open stories" of their lives, stories which allow more to be said as life unfolds. Directors help people to develop their own life stories, to be imaginative, and to come to new understandings of events. This process helps men and women to go beyond a closed story with its rigid interpretation of self, world, and God. Such rigid interpretation is often a symptom of midlife crisis. People with open stories can continue to hear the Gospel story with open ears and open hearts. The sacred stories still suggest new interpretations, new possibilities to them. The sacred dimension of their personal story is apprehended from new and different angles.[97]

A person coming to direction is invited to reflect on his or her present way of living in light of the Christian story. The invitation is to engage in a process of critical reflection as he or she inquires about past influences and future goals. In this process one's life story is more clearly revealed, and the reflection becomes a catalyst for change, inasmuch as insight into the story suggests new images for self. Dialogue between the self and the life story as well as that between the person and the director facilitates the movement toward a clearer vision for the future.[98]

In this dialogue both storytelling *and* listening are vitally important. As people hear themselves telling their own stories, they gain a new perspective on what is going on in their lives. The director, by an attentive attitude and by carefully formulated questions, helps people get in touch with lost, confused, or misunderstood facets of their stories as well as with their sacred dimension. In some cases the director may relate people's experiences to the sacred stories of the Scriptures and so lead them to new interpretations of what has been and is going on in their lives. But such explicit connections need not always be made, for besides the speaker and the director, there is also a third listener to all that is being said. Douglas Steere has written beautifully about "the hidden presence, the patient, all-penetrating Listener, the third member of every conversation whose very existence, if it is not ignored, rebukes and damps down the evil and calls out and underlines the good, drawing from the visible participants things they did not know they possessed."[99]

Direction at midlife ultimately leads to the establishment of a deep and vital relationship with that eternal Listener. It is in dialogue with that Listener that one's identity is grounded in the experience of being loved beyond any human imagining. When one's identity is rooted in faith in the God who meets the deepest desires of the human heart, there comes a renewed zest for life. Struggles will continue, limitations still have to be accepted, death must be faced, but care—a continued investment in life and a transcendence of self—becomes the only viable response. "In this is love, not that we loved God but that he loved us and sent his Son to be the expiation for our sins. Beloved, if God so loved us, we also ought to love one another. No man has ever seen God; if we love one another, God abides in us and his love is perfected in us" (I Jn 4: 10–12).

Notes to Chapter Four

1. The human heart as the place where God chooses to dwell is often mentioned in the history of Christian spirituality. For example, a fourteenth century meditation on the Resurrection describes the Lord speaking to Mary Magdalene at the empty tomb: "Woman, why are you weeping? Whom are you looking for? The one you seek is in your possession, and you do not know it? You have the true, the eternal joy, and yet you weep? It is within your inmost being, and you look for it without? You stand outside, weeping at the tomb. Your heart is my tomb. And I am not dead there, but I take my rest in your heart, living for ever. Your soul is my garden. You were right to suppose that I was the gardener. I am the New Adam. I till and mind my paradise. Your tears, your love and your longing are all my work. In your inmost being you possess me, although you do not know it, and so you look for me without. Outwardly, therefore, I will appear to you, and so make you return to yourself, that in your inmost being you may find the one whom you seek outside." Cited and translated in Andre Louf, *Teach Us to Pray*, trans. by Hubert Hoskins (New York: Paulist Press, 1975), pp. 38–39.

2. See the discussion of patristic notions of reform in Gerhart B. Ladner, *The Idea of Reform: Its Impact on Christian Thought and Action in the Age of the Fathers* (Cambridge, Mass.: Harvard University Press, 1959), esp. Part 2, "The Early Christian Idea of Reform."

3. *The Scale of Perfection*, abridged and presented by Illtyd Trethowan (St. Meinrad, Ind.: Abbey Press, 1975), Bk. I, chaps. 48, 49, pp. 50–51.

4. *Ibid.*, Bk. II, chap. 30, p. 98.

5. C. G. Jung, *Aion: Researches into the Phenomenology of the Self*, 2nd ed., trans. by R. F. C. Hull, Bollingen Series 20 (Princeton, N.J.: Princeton University Press, 1959), p. 40.

6. Urban T. Holmes III, *Ministry and Imagination* (New York: Seabury, 1976), p. 95.

7. "Is the Contemplative Life Finished?" in *Contemplation in a World of Action*, p. 357.

8. See Ray L. Hart, *The Unfinished Man and the Imagination* (New York: Herder and Herder, 1968), p. 225.

9. David Baily Harned, *Images for Self-Recognition: The Christian as Player, Sufferer, and Vandal* (New York: Seabury, 1977), p. 2.

10. *The Future of an Illusion*, trans. by W. D. Robson-Scott, revised and ed. by James Strachey (Garden City, N.Y.: Anchor Books, 1964), p. 49. Also see Paul W. Pruyser's discussion of illusion in *Between Belief and Unbelief*, pp. 196–205.

11. "The Psychology of Religious Experience," *Communio*, 4 (1977), 52.

12. Holmes, pp. 100, 109.

13. *Basic Selections from Emerson* (New York: New American Library, 1954); this passage is cited and discussed in Paul C. Horton, *Solace: The*

Missing Dimension in Psychiatry (Chicago and London: University of Chicago Press, 1981), p. 116.

14. Trans. by John W. Harvey (Oxford: Oxford University Press, 1950), pp. 146–47.

15. "Listening to the Parables of Jesus," in *The Philosophy of Paul Ricoeur: An Anthology of His Work*, ed. by Charles E. Regan and David Stewart (Boston: Beacon Press, 1978), p. 241.

16. *Ibid.*, p. 245.

17. "Forms and Functions of the Imagination in Religion," (photocopy), pp. 15–16.

18. "Transitional Objects and Transitional Phenomena," in *Playing and Reality* (New York: Basic Books, 1971), pp. 1–25. See also Madeleine Davis and David Wallbridge, *Boundary and Space: An Introduction to the Work of D. W. Winnicott* (New York: Brunner/Mazel, 1981); and *Between Reality and Fantasy: Transitional Objects and Phenomena*, ed. by Simon A. Grolnick and Leonard Barkin in collaboration with Werner Muensterberger (New York: Jason Aronson, 1978).

19. Emilie Sobel, "Rhythm, Sound and Imagery in the Poetry of Gerard Manley Hopkins," in *Between Reality and Fantasy*, p. 428.

20. *Playing and Reality*, p. 3.

21. "The Psychology of Religious Experience," p. 52.

22. *Between Belief and Unbelief*, pp. 111–12.

23. Pruyser, "Forms and Functions of the Imagination in Religion," p. 29.

24. *Ibid.*

25. See Paul W. Pruyser, "An Essay on Creativity," *Bulletin of the Menninger Clinic*, 43 (1979), 294–353, esp. 329–31.

26. See Matthias Neuman, "Self-Identity, Symbol, and Imagination: Some Implications of Their Interaction for Christian Sacramental Theology," in *Symbolisme et Théologie: Sacramentum 2* (Rome: Editrice Anselmiana, 1975), pp. 92–97.

27. "Elements of a Psychoanalytic Theory of Psychosocial Development," in *The Course of Life: Psychoanalytic Contributions Toward Understanding Personality Development*, Vol. 1, *Infancy and Early Childhood*, ed. by Stanley I. Greenspan and George H. Pollock (Washington, D.C.: US Government Printing Office, 1980), pp. 41–42.

28. See the fine discussion of images of self and their power in Alan Jones, *Exploring Spiritual Direction*, pp. 83–98.

29. See Mardi Jon Horowitz, *Image Formation and Psychotherapy* (New York: Jason Aronson, 1983), pp. 87–88.

30. See Paul Ricoeur, *Freud and Philosophy: An Essay on Interpretation*, trans. by Denis Savage (New Haven: Yale University Press, 1970), pp. 494–97 where Ricoeur discusses a hermeneutics of retrieval as one approach to symbols. For a discussion of self-images as symbols see Neuman, p. 100

where he observes: "Every self-image is a symbol; it encases a number of directions and meanings."

31. See the excellent treatment of such distractions in prayer in Ann and Barry Ulanov, *Primary Speech: A Psychology of Prayer* (Atlanta: John Knox Press, 1982), pp. 35–43.

32. *Ibid.*, p. 38.

33. *Images of Hope: Imagination As Healer of the Hopeless* (Notre Dame, Ind.: University of Notre Dame Press, 1974), p. 196.

34. *The Wisdom of the Desert*, pp. 56–57.

35. See Gerald G. May, *Care of Mind/Care of Spirit*, pp. 81–82; Calvin F. Settlage, "Cultural Values and the Superego in Late Adolescence," *The Psychoanalytic Study of the Child*, 27 (1972), 90–91; M. Scott, Peck, *The Road Less Traveled*, pp. 69–72.

36. See George W. Stroup, *The Promise of Narrative Theology: Recovering the Gospel in the Church* (Atlanta: John Knox, 1981), pp. 101–107.

37. Hans W. Loewald, *Psychoanalysis and the History of the Individual* (New Haven: Yale University Press, 1978), pp. 21–22.

38. See Paul Ricoeur, *Interpretation Theory: Discourse and the Surplus of Meaning* (Fort Worth, Tex.: Texas Christian University Press, 1976), pp. 79, 94; *idem, Hermeneutics and the Human Sciences: Essays on Language, Action and Interpretation*, ed. and trans. by John B. Thompson (Cambridge: Cambridge University Press, 1981), pp. 56–57, 220–21; and Robert S. Steele, *Freud and Jung: Conflicts of Interpretation* (London: Routledge & Kegan Paul, 1982), p. 347.

39. See Steele, p. 348; and Holmes, pp. 98–99.

40. "Psychology and Hermeneutics: An Exploration of Basic Issues and Resources," *Journal of Religion*, 55 (1975), 327–47.

41. Ricoeur, *Freud and Philosophy*, p. 496 where Ricoeur describes two hermeneutics: "one turned toward the revival of archaic meanings belonging to the infancy of mankind, the other turned toward the emergence of figures that anticipate our spiritual adventure."

42. See Neuman, p. 100.

43. *The Symbolism of Evil*, trans. by Emerson Buchanan (New York: Harper & Row, 1967), pp. 14–17. There is a variety of approaches to the nature and meaning of symbols. Clifford Geertz categorizes as symbols "tangible formulations of notions, abstractions from experience fixed in perceptible forms, concrete embodiments of ideas, attitudes, judgments, longings, or beliefs"; see "Religion as a Cultural System" in *The Interpretation of Culture* (New York: Basic Books, 1973), p. 91. Avery Dulles, in writing of the symbolic mediation of revelation, states: "A symbol is a sign pregnant with a plenitude of meaning which is evoked rather than explicitly stated"; see *Models of Revelation* (Garden City, N.Y.: Doubleday, 1983), p. 132.

44. See Burrell, "The Church and Individual Life," in *Toward Vatican III*, pp. 125–26.

45. See Jones, pp. 86–90.

46. H. Richard Niebuhr, *The Responsible Self: An Essay in Christian Moral Philosophy* (New York: Harper & Row, 1963), p. 156.

47. *Psychology and Religion: West and East*, Bollingen Series 11 (New York: Pantheon Books, 1958), p. 273.

48. *Ibid.*, p. 157.

49. Jolande Jacobi, *Complex-Archetype-Symbol in the Psychology of C. G. Jung*, trans. by Ralph Manheim, Bollingen Series 57 (New York: Pantheon Books, 1959), p. 88.

50. Arnold van Gennep, *The Rites of Passage* (Chicago: University of Chicago Press, 1960), pp. 10–11.

51. The anthropologist Victor Turner's study of liminality would throw further light on the experience of individuals at midlife. In designating various types of "liminal people," he remarks: "Prophets and artists tend to be liminal and marginal people, 'edgemen,' who strive with a passionate sincerity to rid themselves of the clichés associated with status incumbency and role-playing and to enter into vital relations with other men in fact or imagination. In their productions we may catch glimpses of that unused evolutionary potential in mankind which has not yet been externalized and fixed in structure." *The Ritual Process: Structure and Anti-Structure* (Chicago: Aldine Publishing Company, 1969), p. 128; see also "Passages, Margins, and Poverty: Religious Symbols of Communitas," in *Dramas, Fields, and Metaphors: Symbolic Action in Human Society* (Ithaca and London: Cornell University Press, 1974), pp. 231–71.

52. Searle, "The Journey of Conversion," p. 47.

53. *Zen in the Art of Archery*, trans. by R. F. C. Hull (New York: Vintage Books, 1971), p. 58.

54. Gerald G. May, *Will and Spirit: A Contemplative Psychology* (San Francisco: Harper & Row, 1982), p. 6. May provides an extensive discussion of willingness and willfulness in his book; see pp. 1–22.

55. See Harned, pp. 6–8.

56. *Ibid.*, pp. 43–60.

57. Niebuhr, p. 167.

58. "The responsible Christian is . . . accountable not only to the community of faith but also to the universal community and to its Lord. The universal frame of reference is the whole within which the individual finds meaning as a part." Spohn, p. 37 where the author is relating Niebuhr's notion of the self as responder to the issue of Christian moral discernment.

59. (New York: Vintage Books, 1973), p. 265.

60. *Ibid.*, p. 263.

61. *Ibid.*, p. 265.

62. *Contemplative Prayer* (Garden City, N.Y.: Image Books, 1971), p. 70.

63. See Thomas Acklin, "The Imaginative Interplay of the Self Image and the Image of God," *New Catholic World*, 225 (1982), 269–72.

64. *The Religious Imagination* (New York: Sadlier, 1981), p. 3.

119

65. "The Psychology of Religious Experience," 53.

66. "Some Reflections on Schoolboy Psychology," *Standard Edition*, 13, p. 243.

67. See the discussion of Freud's contribution to the study of God-images in Ana-Maria Rizzuto, *The Birth of the Living God: A Psychoanalytic Study* (Chicago and London: University of Chicago Press, 1979), pp. 13–37.

68. *Freud and the Problem of God*, trans. by Edward Quinn (New Haven: Yale University Press, 1979), p. 98.

69. *Care of Mind/Care of Spirit*, p. 66.

70. Rizzuto, p. 7.

71. *Ibid.*, p. 46.

72. Gerald May wisely observes: "Spiritual direction should, whenever possible, focus on that heartfelt sense beneath the imagery, and deal with minor image-distortions only when they can be identified as causing real problems. In other words, the realization that some image-distortions exist should not cause one to immediately embark on a crusade to correct them all." *Care of Mind/Care of Spirit*, p. 62. For remarks on prayer as a means of relating consciously to a God-image, see Ann Ulanov, review of *The Birth of the Living God: A Psychoanalytic Study*, by Ana-Maria Rizzuto, *Union Seminary Quarterly Review*, 36 (1981), 175.

73. See Kathleen R. Fischer, *The Inner Rainbow: The Imagination in Christian Life* (New York: Paulist Press, 1983), pp. 110–23.

74. See Paul W. Pruyser, "Narcissism in Contemporary Religion," *Journal of Pastoral Care*, 32 (1978), 219–31, esp. pp. 220–21. Thomas Acklin remarks: "The symbolic figure of God proposed within Christian cultures calls the human imagination to image him in a way that draws the imagination beyond a God imaged merely according to the self's own image and likeness, to a God who is as really other to the self as any other in reality." Acklin, p. 272.

75. See W. W. Meissner, "Psychoanalytic Aspects of Religious Experience," 126–141.

76. This section is based on a chart by Rizzuto which correlates the individual's sense of self with successive reworkings of the God-image. In this chart she ascribes these particular changes in sense of self and God-image to senescence, but the revised sense of self at midlife would suggest a stance toward the God-image similar to what she posits for advanced age. See Rizzuto, pp. 206–207.

77. Merton, *Contemplative Prayer*, pp. 77–78.

78. "Religion in Relation to Personal Integration," *British Journal of Medical Psychology*, 42 (1969), 331.

79. Stanley Hauerwas, *Truthfulness and Tragedy* (Notre Dame, Ind.: University of Notre Dame Press, 1977), p. 76.

80. "The Narrative Quality of Experience," *Journal of the American Academy of Religion*, 39 (1971), 300.

81. See Eugene W. King, "A Pastoral Theological Reflection on Storytelling," *Chicago Studies*, 21 (1982), 8–11; and Holmes, p. 166.

82. "Time, Age, and the Life Cycle," p. 893.

83. See J. R. Wilkes, "Remembering," *Theology*, 84 (1981), 89.

84. See Steele, pp. 370–372.

85. *Ibid.*, p. 350.

86. See Walter Lowe, "Psychoanalysis as an Archeology of the History of Suffering," in *The Challenge of Psychology to Faith*, Concilium, 156, ed. by Steven Kepnes and David Tracy (New York: Seabury, 1982), pp. 3–9; and Alice Miller, *Prisoners of Childhood*, trans. by Ruth Ward (New York: Basic Books, 1981).

87. See Evelyn Eaton Whitehead and James D. Whitehead, *Christian Life Patterns: The Psychological Challenges and Religious Invitations of Adult Life*, pp. 185–187; and Charles R. Stinnette, Jr., "Reflection and Transformation: Knowing and Change in Psychotherapy and in Religious Faith," in *The Dialogue Between Theology and Psychology*, Essays in Divinity, III, ed. by Peter Homans (Chicago: University of Chicago Press, 1968), pp. 102–106.

88. *Time and Myth* (Notre Dame, Ind.: University of Notre Dame Press, 1975), p. 81.

89. Crites, p. 295.

90. Spohn, "The Reasoning Heart: An American Approach to Christian Discernment," p. 39.

91. King, p. 17.

92. John Shea, *Stories of God: An Unauthorized Biography* (Chicago: Thomas More Press, 1978), p. 164; see pp. 89–101 for a discussion of the interventionist interpretation.

93. *Ibid.*, pp. 152–53; see pp. 101–16 for Shea's presentation of intentional interpretation.

94. See Dermot A. Lane, *The Experience of God: An Invitation to Do Theology* (New York: Paulist Press, 1981), esp. pp. 15–17; 63–66.

95. Shea, p. 186.

96. Spohn, p. 42.

97. See Holmes, pp. 166–68.

98. See Thomas H. Groome, *Christian Religious Education: Sharing Our Story and Vision* (San Francisco: Harper & Row, 1980), pp. 184–197 where Groome describes what he sees as the components of a shared praxis approach to religious education. There is strong affinity between his suggestions and the approach to spiritual direction at midlife suggested here. In fact, when religious education is seen as the nurturing of faith and a fostering of continuing conversion, it can be legitimately seen as a form of group spiritual direction. However, Groome's ideas are here related to the one-to-one experience of direction.

99. "On Listening to Another," in *The Doubleday Devotional Classics*, Vol. III, ed. by E. Glenn Hinson (Garden City, N.Y.: Doubleday, 1978), pp. 222–23.

CHAPTER FIVE

Guidelines for Direction of Midlife Adults

"The virtuous soul that is alone and without a master, is like a lone burning coal; it will grow colder rather than hotter. . . . If you do not fear falling alone, how do you presume that you will rise up alone? Consider how much more can be accomplished by two together than by one alone."[1] By these and other maxims John of the Cross underscores the importance of spiritual direction for growth in love and holiness. The acquired wisdom of a good director becomes a resource for those struggling with doubt and confusion about the direction in which they should move. The director helps those at midlife to assess where they are and where the Spirit is inviting them. Such guidance fosters conversion and discernment and stimulates the imagination. It is based on the director's own experiences.

Nothing in life is a total waste. Any personal experience—bad or good—can serve as "material" for the observant spiritual director. Skilled directors are able to draw on the accumulated data and wisdom in their own lives. Experiences of spiritual direction undertaken for their own development often serve as resources for what can be truly helpful to others in following the leads of the Spirit. Study and prayer continue to open directors up to new approaches and to make them more perceptive to the subtleties of the spiritual life. As facilitators of religious development, however, directors believe that the purpose of the direction relationship is to foster a person's growth in sensitivity to the Eternal Listener's presence in his or her life.

The vast spiritual tradition itself provides directors with examples of men and women who have effectively guided others; it also provides models for good spiritual direction today. These historical models may reveal deficiencies in a director's previous experiences, or they may reenforce the conclusions he or she has drawn from beneficial, growth-producing experiences of direction. The tradition, moreover, underscores certain aspects in the direction relationship which can serve as guidelines for its practice with people at midlife. Most of these key elements are further supported by the conclusions of those engaged in therapy and analysis or in other helping professions. We shall offer seven of these guidelines here as the practical conclusion of what we have presented throughout these pages.

1 *The direction relationship aims to facilitate ongoing conversion at midlife. Warmth and friendliness make adjustment possible*

The quality of the relationship which directors establish with people at midlife is one of the most important factors in the direction process. In the context of a trusting relationship directees are enabled to sort out their lives and move toward the future to which the Spirit invites them. The importance of establishing such a relationship with a wise person in order to grow in the spiritual life is amply supported in the long tradition of spirituality.

We have noted that in the early Christian era many people went out to the deserts of Egypt, Syria, and Palestine to find spiritual guides to foster their growth and development. In this desert tradition several features of the direction relationship stand out clearly. Openness and directness are foremost. The masters indeed would teach, but not in the sense of imparting intellectual knowledge ("which I have and you don't"). Their manner of teaching was analogous to what a music teacher might do to help a person to play an instrument or to sing. They imparted or shared a method for using the talents which were God-given and already present.

As effective discerners of the Spirit in their own lives, these "masters" would listen to the stories of their "disciples," which were replete with all the concerns which make any person's story unique as well as the struggles which are part of every person's lot. The comments of the masters were brief and to the point. They were received by the disciples as life-giving words. These words with their fresh perspective brought liberation to persons who were weighted down by struggle and conflict. The words did not usually take away the difficulty. They did, however, make it more bearable by giving it meaning and value in the overall process of growth and development.[2]

One of the women of the desert, Theodora, spoke about the qualities needed: "A teacher ought to be a stranger to the desire for domination, vain-glory, and pride; one should not be able to fool him [or her] by flattery, nor blind him [or her] by gifts, nor conquer by the stomach, nor dominate him [or her] by anger; but he [or she] should be patient, gentle and humble as far as possible; he [or she] must be tested and without partisanship, full of concern, and a lover of souls."[3] Direction is about genuine human relationships. A mature relationship is present when unreasonable expectations are set aside. Such a relationship exists where two people are aware of their own uniqueness and responsibility, and where trust and love provide an atmosphere for open and honest communication. Directing another person demands readiness for mature relationships and all that that involves.

Francis de Sales (1567–1622) emphasized the friendly tone of the direction relationship. In his time direction usually took place in the context of sacramental confession. Consequently his remarks are directed to confessors, but they apply to contemporary directors as well. Claiming that friendship provides the best context for growth and development, he counsels those engaged in this ministry to strive to be friends with those who come to them and to let themselves be loved as persons. The relationship which De Sales describes is reciprocal; the one seeking counsel is likewise to approach the minister with the confidence that one would place in a friend.[4]

De Sales' approach is indirect, and it allows people a major role in ascertaining what God is asking in their conversion. This approach bolsters the self-esteem and sense of dignity of the people who come for direction. It recognizes their uniqueness and allows them to follow the pattern of growth proper to their unique selves. De Sales paid attention to people's feelings and appealed to them as a means of strengthening the will in its quest for God. He would elicit positive feelings not only toward such things as the suffering of Christ but also toward himself as minister and friend as a way of drawing people toward God. This affective method was indicative of De Sales' genius. It contributed to his success in drawing the whole person into the sphere of God's merciful love.[5]

Good direction flows from the experience of solid human relationships as well as from the experiential knowledge of the difficulties which everyone faces in entering into such relationships. Like the spiritual masters of the past, today's directors are vested with a certain authority in virtue of their knowledge and skill in the spiritual life. The professional distance which results and is appropriate does not preclude warmth and friendship. In the helpful climate of relationships to directors—some long-lasting, others regrettably short—people can come to terms with the expectations they have of others, of themselves, and of God.

2 *In the spiritual direction relationship both sides (but especially the director) need to be aware of possible hidden agendas, unrealistic expectations, and the elements that can vitiate growth*

At some point a directee may want the director to tell him or her exactly what to do; he or she may expect the director to take away all pain and struggle. These expectations can come from childhood and may still color many of an individual's interactions with significant people. Because these expectations determine a child's perceptions of the self and others, later in life they can prevent a person from accepting a fully responsible adult status in the Church and in life.

The surrender of unrealizable childhood expectations is an important aspect of the growth which is sought in spiritual direction and in other helping processes. In psychoanalytic treatment, changing childhood patterns of relating with others into appropriate adult patterns is a major part of the work. These childhood patterns are identified as they make their appearance in the relationship between patient and analyst. Analysts refer to the emergence of these patterns as "transference." As the analyst Harry Guntrip has noted, "Freud . . . discovered that one of the things that happens to repressed experiences in childhood is that later in life the emotions find an outlet by transference onto some roughly analogous figure in the present day. This phenomenon of 'transference'—so prolific a cause of disruption in friendships, marriages, and adult partnerships of all kinds—inevitably erupts, unrecognized by the person in the treatment situation. The therapist, then, gets a chance to help the patient gradually to recognize and grow out of these survivals of past experience to become free to relate in emotionally realistic and appropriate ways to people in the present day."[6]

Midlife may require people to come to terms with a secret desire to be taken care of by someone (for example, the director) as they were cared for earlier in life. Directors, sensitive to the changes which have taken place through the course of their own adult lives, are aware of how difficult it is to surrender such expectations. Directors meet these patterns in directees not with judgment but with compassion and understanding. They give space for learning, since they know their own struggles in coming to fuller maturity and wisdom.

Directors, moreover, allow directees to feel their own pain and to learn through it. Facing the pain caused by life's problems can be a maturing experience, and it can draw forth a directee's courage and wisdom to resolve difficulties rather than to deny them. Directors guide people toward a calm acceptance of legitimate suffering. A story from the tradition of desert monasticism illustrates this aspect of the relationship. "It was said of Abba John the Dwarf, that one day he said to his elder brother, 'I should like to be free of all care, like the angels, who do not work, but ceaselessly offer worship to God.' So he took off his cloak and went away into the desert. After a week he came back to his brother. When he knocked on the door, he heard his brother say, before he opened it 'Who are you?' He said, 'I am John, your brother.' But he replied, 'John has become an angel, and henceforth he is no longer among men.' Then the other begged him saying, 'It is I.' However, his brother did not let him in, but left him there in distress until morning. Then, opening the door, he said to him, 'You are a man and you must once again work in order to eat.' "[7]

A director learns to trust in the power of relationships that are therapeutic, liberating, and life-engendering for facilitating change and growth; he or she knows that there are no ready solutions or standard approaches for all cases. The contemporary reflections of analysts and therapists reenforce and elaborate on the traditional wisdom related to the "cure of souls."[8] Guntrip resonates with the ancient tradition when he states: "We do not know what insight we have until we are in the live situation with another human being presenting us with, not a problem to be solved, but an imprisoned self to be understood and freed. Our accumulated experience has made us the actual persons we are right now, and our intuitive understanding of the patient comes, not out of what we intellectually know but out of our capacity to relate, to feel for and with this particular person . . . ."[9]

Directors strive to maintain relationships which will be most helpful to their directees. They need to be aware of their own anger or impatience with directees whenever these present themselves to ensure that these feelings do not have a detrimental effect on the process. Directors will often have to foster a conscious and determined love for the directees. And when sexual feelings surface, they will have to be integrated into a deep concern for the other. "Such feelings are so natural and so spontaneous that some such feelings exist, at least unconsciously, in every spiritual relationship that has sufficient closeness to warrant the name of direction."[10] The experience of a genuine love which is dependable helps a directee to move forward into a life where freedom for the true self is achievable. In such a loving relationship the directee's move to self-acceptance with all his or her past failures and successes is facilitated. God's unconditional love of each individual is reflected in such a relationship.

3   *The director of the midlife adult provides an occasion for the person to tell his or her story*

The compassion which a director offers to a directee creates an atmosphere in which anyone who comes is invited to be more their true selves. But direction relationships are more than friendly chats where directors try to make directees as comfortable as possible. Direction is a working relationship. The directees are expected to do their part: to present their life story. This story will include anything which troubles or consoles the person in his or her relationship with God. It will also include the struggles and joys which are found in prayer, in various relationships, and in the direction relationship itself.

An example from the desert tradition shows how skilful these masters were in facilitating the narrative process so that their disciples could unburden themselves. "Makarios, the most celebrated authority of the Scetic desert, visits the young hermit Theopemtos, whom he knows to be in danger. Joyfully received, the father of monks asks, 'How is it with you?' Afraid to bare himself, the oppressed man replies with a formula of monastic courtesy: 'Due to your prayer it is well.' The old man then asks with greater urgency, 'Are you not being tempted in thought?' But the other insists, 'Up to now I have been well.' Here the old ascetic sheds his dignity. 'See, for many long years I have been practicing self-denial and all men honour me. Yet, though I am old, the daemon of lasciviousness still plagues me, too!' In the same manner, Makarios declares himself exposed to other temptations until he moves the younger one to confession."[11] The end result is a peace of mind that had proved elusive in previous denials.

Similar to Christ's concern for people, directors help people to make sense of their stories in the light of the Kingdom *to come*, yet *already* mysteriously *present*. They exercise a deep caring attitude within the perspective of Christian faith. Care, as Rollo May has described it, is "a state composed of the recognition of another, a fellow human being like one's self; of identification of one's self with the pain or joy of the other; of guilt, pity, and the awareness that we all stand on the base of common humanity from which we all stem."[12] To operate with a faith perspective directors have to have an understanding of their own lives in that same perspective. Their belief in God's involvement in people's lives vitalizes the work of direction and sparks faith in others. As they listen to their directees' stories, directors respond to the Spirit's presence and invite people to a fuller realization of themselves and a discovery of the reality of God.

As he or she invites the telling of a story, the director creates a space where the teller can feel at ease and sense an openness to and acceptance of his or her story. Henri Nouwen has written lucidly about this as hospitality—creating a space where persons can be themselves. "The paradox of hospitality is that it wants to create emptiness—not a fearful emptiness, but a friendly emptiness where strangers can enter and discover themselves as created free . . . free to leave and follow their own vocations. Hospitality is not a subtle invitation to adopt the life style of the host, but the gift of a chance to allow the guest to find his own."[13]

Directors create the friendly, open space where others can discover, as they tell their stories, the direction in which they should move. In the space which direction provides, people grow in sensitivity to their own stories, acknowledge their own past histories, and come to a deeper understanding of them. Witnessing to the primary importance of religious development, directors offer themselves as a frame of reference for the directees' own self-understanding.[14] Through a dialogue of questions and clarifications, directees are enabled to come to a clearer vision of themselves and of God and to incorporate and develop neglected dimensions of themselves. Through the process of putting into words what they see, feel, and believe is happening in their lives, they are able to gain a new perspective on the challenges and promises of midlife.

4   *In the process of midlife spiritual direction, creativity is fostered through a form of adult play. Such creative play often reveals new avenues to growth*

Childhood play is not completely left behind in adulthood. Religious development requires that play continue to be a dimension of human life and that certain features of childhood be preserved in maturity. In the Gospel of Matthew, Jesus remarks:

"Let the children come to me, and do not hinder them; for to such belongs the kingdom of heaven" (19:14). Karl Rahner, commenting on this passage, observes that what is implied is "that we can be like children in being receivers and as such carefree in relation to God, those who *know* that they have nothing of themselves on which to base any claim to his help, and yet who trust that his kindness and protection will be extended to them. . . ."[15]

Childhood is marked by an openness to mystery. When this openness to mystery is preserved in adulthood, life is, in Rahner's words, "a state in which we are open to expect the unexpected, to commit ourselves to the incalculable, a state which endows us with the power still to be able to play, to recognize that the powers presiding over existence are greater than our own designs, and to submit to their control as our deepest good."[16]

Spiritual direction often depends on the ability of the participants to play. In working with people at midlife, directors frequently need to spark the capacity for play in those who come. "Play is a natural expression of the joy of faith, which makes it possible to engage in life, even the hard work of life, as a game that has its own seriousness . . . , and that yet can be enjoyed precisely because the ultimate seriousness of existence lies elsewhere, with God."[17] This dimension of play is nonetheless a serious activity which engages the minds and hearts of those involved. A negative reaction to this aspect of direction in the adult at midlife is often related to associating play with childish activity or with formation in his or her family; this, too, will have to be faced.

The psychoanalyst D. W. Winnicott has pointed out that play throughout a person's life facilitates growth and health. Playing is a natural and universal phenomenon which depends for its beginning in early life on the experience of a trustworthy, reliable environment. Playing goes on in what Winnicott calls "potential space," an intermediate area between one's inner psychic reality and the "object" world in which a person lives. In this potential space the child and later the adult forms a symbolic view of the world. It is also the place where the true self is found. "It is in playing and only in playing that the child or adult is able to be creative and use the whole personality, and it is only in being creative that the individual discovers the self."[18]

Erik Erikson, in studying the relationship between make-believe and belief, has also noted the importance of play. His work is a call for serious playfulness because it is related to the person's basic need for a shared vision of reality. Whereas Winnicott talks about potential space, Erikson speaks of play space as important for human functioning and adaptation: "Play in childhood provides the infantile form of the human propensity to create model situations in which aspects of the past are re-lived, the present re-presented and renewed, and the future anticipated."[19] Spiritual direction is a form of play insofar as its creative dynamics free a person for a fuller life.

In spiritual direction this means a playful handling of the images of self, God, and the world. The atmosphere of trust and compassion makes this possible. Moreover, play pervades most religious activity because it allows and creates the conditions for creatively dealing with a mass of images. Religious rituals are more formalized types of play which provide a respite from the pressures of everyday life and so serve to renew the participants.[20] Play, however, can have a sacred dimension, apart from religious ritual. On this point Paul Pruyser has written: "Playing, because of its transcendence to internal wishes and external facts, is a quasi-sacred activity, a rite around the altar of ideals and meanings which human history has prepared for each new generation. One comes to this altar not to seek a diversion but to replenish oneself, to share in the rites, to experience wonderment, to make one's offerings or pledges, and to feel that one is responsibly in touch with mystery."[21]

Since midlife adults often have to find new ways to be creative, playing helps in the discovery of these avenues. The new vision of life which direction makes possible can awaken dormant talents and reveal exciting challenges which can organize and focus a person's energies. Winnicott has this to say: "It is creative apperception more than anything else that makes the individual feel that life is worth living. Contrasted with this is a relationship to external reality which is one of compliance, the world and its details being recognised but only as something to be fitted in with or demanding adaptation. Compliance carries with it a sense of futility for the individual and is associated with the idea that nothing matters and that life is not worth living. In a tantalizing way many individuals recognize that for most of their time they are living uncreatively, as if caught up in the creativity of someone else, or of a machine."[22]

5 *A spiritual director helps those at midlife to discern among possible visions of life by engaging their imaginations. New perspectives can then emerge*

In the prophecy of Joel, the advent of the Day of the Lord is described as bringing some remarkable blessings. "And it shall come to pass afterward, that I will pour out my spirit on all flesh; your sons and your daughters shall prophesy, your old men shall dream dreams, and your young men shall see visions" (2:28). Peter's Pentecost sermon in the Acts of the Apostles (2:17ff) echoes those words in the event of Jesus. A vision, a dream, is given to Christian people through the outpouring of the Spirit. Spiritual direction enables people to gain a stronger hold on that Christian vision.

The importance of some vision for healthy living is increasingly recognized by researchers and practitioners in various disciplines. Roy Schafer has written about the psychoanalytic vision of reality: "The term *vision* implies judgments partly rooted in subjectivity, that is, in acts of imagination and articles of faith, which, however illuminating and complex they may be, necessarily involve looking at reality from certain angles and not others."[23]

Visions can have comic, romantic, tragic, and ironic features. When people approach the world with their imaginations, one or other of these features may be given special emphais. A comic vision will have a utopian, optimistic quality, and a romantic vision will see life as a series of heroic quests. The tragic vision is especially sensitive to the terrors and absurdities of existence. The Christian vision of life is often depicted as the opposite of the tragic. However, William Lynch has astutely observed: "Far from killing or dissolving the

131

tragic, faith seems to take it as its own special territory, affirming it, confirming it, amplifying it, extending it, deepening it, in order to precisely accomplish its own special objectives."[24] This incorporation of the tragic dimension in the faith vision is especially pertinent at midlife when the tragic, as Elliott Jaques has indicated, comes to the forefront of consciousness. The ironic vision is characterized by an awareness of internal contradictions, paradoxes, and ambiguities. It leads one to a certain detachment and to a tendency to take things less seriously than the tragic vision does.[25] The ironic vision can be especially salutary at midlife.

The value of the ironic vision is that it can hold together seemingly irreconcilable polarities. As Lynch notes: "The shock of irony . . . comes not only from uniting them [apparently irreconcilable polarities] but also from seeing that the act of uniting them is not a mistake. . . . In Christianity there is more than fascinating coexistence of the low and the high. The lowliness is the very instrument to be passed through in order to reach the height. It is also right to say that it *is* the high. And there is more than paradox or ironic brilliance involved. There is an actual transformation of being."[26] Faith is ironic; it is this dimension of reality and vision which directors need to emphasize with those who are at midlife.

The Christian vision of life does not deny the tragic but moves beyond it to the irony of Christ. Directors may meet people at midlife whose comic and romantic visions of life have collapsed and who now find themselves weighed down by the tragic. These people can be prepared for the "imaginative shock" of the Christian paradox. Death and loss remain tragic realities, but a different vision, the vision of faith, can give a new perspective on them. The comprehensive nature of the Christian vision can restore a wholeness to life and lead to the experience of integrity which Erikson has described.

The Christian vision serves as the framework for all that directors do for those who come to them. It is the interpretive tool for understanding the real condition of those who come for assistance. The diagnosis which is done in direction proceeds from a mutual understanding of a person's situation in the perspective of the Christian vision of life. The categories used are those which have emerged from the Christian frame of reference. Consequently, providence, faith, grace, repentance, and vocation are among the central themes in the direction dialogue.[27] Direction is the place where the personal world

132

is woven into the texture of the Christian vision and where new patterns of imagining emerge and creativity is unleashed.[28]

6   *Spiritual direction aims to foster greater tranquility in the midst of life's struggles and challenges*

One of the Gospel accounts presents Jesus walking on the water toward his disciples who were in a boat tossed about by a violent storm (Mt 14:22–33; Mk 6:45–51; Jn 6:16–21). At first the disciples did not recognize him and were terrified. In Matthew's account Peter got out of the boat and began to walk on the water at the Lord's invitation. But when Peter found himself sinking, he was saved by the Lord who reprimanded him for his lack of faith. Jesus got into the boat and the wind died down.

Direction is an exercise which facilitates the deepening of faith. The *Sturm und Drang* of midlife puts faith to the test; fear and doubt beset even the most staunch believers. Faith battles with doubt; when faith is deepened, it is prepared for new encounters with doubt. The experience of midlife for some people can be compared to sinking into a sea of hitherto unnoticed feelings.

As people become aware of the precariousness of their existence, they often search frantically for a savior. Direction provides an opportunity to establish an identity in faith which then becomes the foundation for a creative engagement with life because it focuses on the One who alone can give salvation. As Don Browning has noted: "Faith-identity . . . provides for the believer a stable framework, in the context of which the contingencies of life become more manageable. . . . Faith-identity is the ultimate buffer against the anxiety produced by life's finite and transient character."[29]

In faith a person finds a solid footing for the self in a central relationship to God. Such faith relativizes other sources of affirmation and gives resilience in the face of turmoil. "Faith is a transforming process that touches all parts of the psychic structure and reorganizes them into a pattern that is different and integrates them into a more mature and effective level of function. Faith has, therefore, an integrative function in the psychic economy. True faith is thereby restorative, recuperative, and effectively maturing."[30]

The spiritual masters of the desert helped their disciples to achieve tranquility, that state of final integration attained through purity of heart. Tranquil disciples find the will of God in whatever facilitates their relationship with God. This tranquility is acquired through freeing the self from excessive cares and from preoccupations with one's own importance. Tranquil persons find their true identity as human beings who are made for God.[31]

The tranquil person is one who receives or possesses the Holy Spirit, thus his or her behavior is Spirit-motivated. With this sense of tranquility, a person experiences the presence of the Lord even in the midst of struggle. Tranquil people depend on the Lord to accomplish in them whatever healing integration they lack the power to bring about in themselves. Acceptance of the truth of their real condition leads them to a tranquil integration in the Lord. They have found the ultimate meaning of life and can embrace a vocation to holiness in that particular state in life which is truly and properly theirs. They come to rest in God who is their tranquility.

In the final pages of Greene's *A Burnt-Out Case*, the architect Querry remarks: "I suppose belief is a kind of vocation . . . If we really believe in something we have no choice, have we, but to go further. Otherwise life slowly whittles the belief away. My architecture stood still. One can't be a half-believer or a half-architect."[32] Spiritual direction tries to help people go further in their belief. For those at midlife, it sharpens the faith vision and helps to overcome the stagnation which may have occurred. Tranquility grows out of wholehearted, growing faith and the willingness to overcome the obstacles to it.

Tranquility is not easy to come by, but it can be gradually achieved through the often painful process of discernment with the help of a director. Through the sharing of their stories, feelings, and thoughts in direction, people learn to distinguish the pull of evil in themselves from the genuine movement of God's grace. They learn to separate their own pride, vanity, or obsessive fantasies from their perception of God's will. False assertiveness, defensiveness, and false passivity can be identified and faced creatively in the direction relationship. Those who persevere acquire the confidence and freedom that comes to humble people, to those who place their trust in God.

People usually emerge from the experience of direction with a unified vision of life, a sense of having touched the inner core of reality. With this view of life, they are able to bring perspective, freedom, and spontaneity into the lives of others. They become peacemakers by fostering the unity of their many communities. The tranquil person, no longer preoccupied with self, can care for others and feel their joys and sorrows without being overwhelmed by them.

7   *Spiritual direction is ultimately the work of the Holy Spirit and an occasion for the experience of God's grace*

In the Last Discourse in John's Gospel, Jesus says to his disciples: "This much have I told you while I was still with you; the Paraclete, the Holy Spirit whom the Father will send in my name, will instruct you in everything, and remind you of all that I told you" (14:25–26). Remembering is the work of the Spirit. The Spirit enables people to make inspired connections between their personal stories and the story of Jesus. In spiritual direction making these connections is often commonplace. Directors learn to trust not in the power of their own insight but in the presence of the unifying Spirit who draws the disparate pieces of an individual's life into a whole.

Karl Rahner has presented a long list of human experiences which could be recognized as experiences of the Spirit. Included in his list are many items which take place in the context of spiritual direction: "When the sum total of all life's accounts, which we cannot work out ourselves, is seen as good by an incomprehensible 'other,' although this cannot be 'proved,' . . . when the bitter, disappointing, and fleeting monotony of ordinary life is borne with serene resignation up to its accepted end out of a strength whose ultimate source cannot be grasped and so cannot be brought under our control,. . . *then* God is present with his liberating grace. Then we experience what we Christians describe as the Holy Spirit of God . . . ."[33]

A skilled and effective director draws people's attention to the presence of the Spirit in human experience. He or she helps people to notice how God's grace has not been absent from their lives and how they are to cherish and remember those gracious moments, memorable moments which will bring them strength in time of difficulty.[34] Empowered by memories of God's past involvement in their lives, people will believe more deeply in God's constant love for them.

The Scriptures repeatedly reinforce this belief in God's never failing presence. In the prophet Hosea, Yahweh proclaims:

> When Israel was a child, I loved him, and out of Egypt I called my son. The more I called them, the more they went from me; they kept

sacrificing to the Baals and burning incense to idols. Yet it was I who taught Ephraim to walk, I took them up in my arms; but they did not know that I healed them. I led them with cords of compassion, with the bands of love, and I became to them as one who eases the yokes on their jaws, and I bent down to them and fed them. How can I give you up, O Ephraim! How can I hand you over, O Israel! (11:1–4, 8).

The director is often called upon to function as a reminder of what God has done and is doing in a person's life. Henri Nouwen has written of the minister from precisely this angle. He discusses the minister as *The Living Reminder*—who heals, sustains, and guides a person in the memory of Jesus Christ. In the epilogue to this book Nouwen sums up in traditional categories what he has said: "As pastors, ministers heal the wounds of the past; as priests, they sustain life in the present; and as prophets, they guide others to the future. They do all of this in memory of him who is, who was, and is to come."[35] This is what a spiritual director does with those at midlife as well as with those at other stages.

The transformation which people undergo in the process of direction is the work of the Spirit. And directors have the privilege of witnessing it. The Spirit can negate the experience of boredom and stagnation and raise individuals to a new level of existence. The puzzles of life, although perhaps not solved, can be lived with, as a new and larger perspective is adopted under the Spirit's guidance. "When the Spirit of truth comes, he will guide you into all the truth; for he will not speak on his own authority, but whatever he hears he will speak, and he will declare to you the things that are to come" (Jn 16:13). This is, after all, what *spiritual* direction is all about. New life is generated. A new man or a new woman can act in his or her world with integrity and purpose. This is the power of grace. And it moves mountains.

Notes to Chapter Five

1. "Sayings of Light and Love," in *The Collected Works of St. John of the Cross*, p. 667.

2. See H. Dörries, "The Place of Confession in Ancient Monasticism," in *Studia Patristica*, Vol. 5, ed. by F. L. Cross (Berlin: Akademie-Verlag, 1962), pp. 284–311.

3. *The Sayings of the Desert Fathers: The Alphabetical Collection*, trans. by Benedicta Ward (London: A. R. Mowbray, 1975), p. 72.

4. See Francis de Sales, *Introduction to the Devout Life*, trans. by John K. Ryan (Garden City, N.Y.: Image Books, 1955), pp. 41–43; and also Raymond Studzinski, "The Minister of Reconciliation: Some Historical Models," in *Background and Directions, The Rite of Penance: Commentaries*, Vol. 3, ed. by Nathan Mitchell (Washington: The Liturgical Conference, 1978), pp. 58–59 where this writer has applied De Sales' teaching to the ministry of sacramental penance.

5. See the discussion of Francis de Sales in Erik Berggren, *The Psychology of Confession* (Leiden: Brill, 1975), pp. 50–56.

6. *Psychoanalytic Theory, Therapy, and the Self: A Basic Guide to the Human Personality in Freud, Erikson, Klein, Sullivan, Fairbairn, Hartmann, Jacobson, and Winnicott* (New York: Basic Books, 1973), p. 9; see the discussion of transference in spiritual direction in May, *Care of Mind/Care of Soul*, pp. 103–108.

7. *The Sayings of the Desert Fathers*, trans. by Ward, p. 73.

8. For a classic investigation of the tradition surrounding the cure of souls, see John T. McNeill, *A History of the Cure of Souls* (New York: Harper & Row, 1951).

9. Guntrip, p. 184.

10. May, *Care of Mind/Care of Soul*, p. 111; May provides an excellent treatment of sexual feelings in direction, see pp. 110–122.

11. Cited in Dörries, p. 288.

12. *Love and Will* (New York: Dell, 1969), p. 285.

13. "Hospitality," *Monastic Studies*, 10 (1974), 8.

14. See Nouwen's remarks on counseling as a form of hospitality, *ibid.*, pp. 19–21.

15. "Ideas for a Theology of Childhood," in *Theological Investigations*, Vol. 8, *Further Theology of the Spiritual Life 2*, trans. by David Bourke (New York: Herder and Herder, 1971), p. 41.

16. *Ibid.*, p. 42.

17. William J. Bouwsma, "Christian Adulthood," in *Adulthood*, ed. by Erik H. Erikson, p. 92.

18. "Playing: Creative Activity and the Search for the Self," in *Playing and Reality*, p. 54.

19. *Toys and Reasons: Stages in the Ritualization of Experience* (New York: W. W. Norton, 1977), p. 44.

20. See Gerhard Marcel Martin, *Fest: The Transformation of Everyday*, trans. by M. Douglas Meeks (Philadelphia: Fortress Press, 1976), pp. 54–58; Andrew Greeley, *Religion: A Secular Theory* (New York: Free Press, 1982), pp. 113–115.

21. "An Essay on Creativity," *Bulletin of the Menninger Clinic*, 43 (1979), 338.

22. "Creativity and its Origins," in *Playing and Reality*, p. 65.

23. *A New Language for Psychoanalysis* (New Haven: Yale University Press, 1976), p. 23.

24. William Lynch, *Images of Faith: An Exploration of the Ironic Imagination* (Notre Dame, Ind.: University of Notre Dame Press, 1973), p. 167.

25. Schafer, pp. 55–56.

26. Lynch, *Images of Faith*, p. 85.

27. See Paul W. Pruyser, *The Minister as Diagnostician*, pp. 60–79.

28. See Davis and Wallbridge, *Boundary and Space*, p. 175 where the authors make this point with reference to what takes place in Winnicott's potential space. Jung spoke of the process of opening oneself to images as the "active imagination." Employing the active imagination creates opportunities for claiming energies and freedom which may have never been realized before. See C. G. Jung, *Analytical Psychology: Its Theory and Practice* (New York: Random House, 1970), pp. 192 ff; Barbara Hannah, *Encounter with the Soul: Active Imagination as Developed by C. G. Jung* (Santa Monica, Cal: Sigo Press, 1981); and Morton Kelsey, *Christo-Psychology* (New York: Crossroad, 1982), pp. 139–52.

29. "Faith and the Dynamics of Knowing," in *The Dialogue Between Theology and Psychology*, ed. by Peter Homans, Essays in Divinity, III (Chicago: University of Chicago Press, 1968), p. 128; see also W. W. Meissner, "Notes on the Psychology of Faith," *Journal of Religion and Health*, 8 (1969), 66–69.

30. Meissner, "Notes on the Psychology of Faith," p. 70.

31. Thomas Merton speaks about the concept of tranquility in his essay "The Spiritual Father in the Desert Tradition," in *Contemplation in a World of Action*, pp. 282–305.

32. Greene, p. 240.

33. "Experience of the Holy Spirit," in *Theological Investigations*, Vol. 18, *God and Revelation*, trans. by Edward Quinn (New York: Crossroad, 1983), pp. 202–203.

34. See the Whiteheads' discussion of anamnesis and the life review in *Christian Life Patterns*, pp. 215–217.

35. *The Living Reminder: Service and Prayer in Memory of Jesus Christ* (New York: Seabury, 1977), p. 75.

Bibliography

Acklin, Thomas. "The Imaginative Interplay of the Self Image and the Image of God." *New Catholic World*, 225 (1982), 269–72.

Alexander, Gary T. "Psychological Foundations of William James's Theory of Religious Experience." *Journal of Religion*, 59 (1979), 421–34.

Athanasius. *The Life of Antony and the Letter to Marcellinus*. Trans. by Robert C. Gregg. New York: Paulist Press, 1980.

Bacht, Heinrich. "Benedikt und Ignatius." In *Benedikt und Ignatius*. Ed. by T. Bogler. Maria Laach, 1963. Pp. 9–30.

____. "Early Monastic Elements in Ignatian Spirituality: Toward Clarifying Some Fundamental Concepts of the Exercises." In *Ignatius of Loyola: His Personality and Spiritual Heritage, 1556–1956*. Ed. by Friedrich Wulf. St. Louis: Institute of Jesuit Sources, 1977. Pp. 200–36.

Barnhouse, Ruth Tiffany. "Spiritual Direction and Psychotherapy." *Journal of Pastoral Care*, 33 (1979), 149–63.

Barry, William A., and Connolly, William J. *The Practice of Spiritual Direction*. New York: Seabury, 1982.

Becker, Ernest. *The Denial of Death*. New York: Free Press, 1973.

Begheyn, Paul. "A Bibliography on St. Ignatius' *Spiritual Exercises*: A Working Tool for American Students." *Studies in the Spirituality of Jesuits*, 13 (1981), no. 2.

Benedict. *RB 1980: The Rule of St. Benedict in Latin and English with Notes*. Ed. By Timothy Fry *et al.* Collegeville, Minn.: Liturgical Press, 1981.

Berggren, Erik. *The Psychology of Confession*. Leiden: Brill, 1975.

Bouwsma, William J. "Christian Adulthood." In *Adulthood*. Ed. by Erik H. Erikson. New York: W. W. Norton, 1978. Pp. 81–96.

Brenan, Gerald. *St. John of the Cross: His Life and Poetry*. With a translation of his poetry by Lynda Nicholson. Cambridge: Cambridge University Press, 1975.

Brewi, Janice, and Brennan, Anne. *Mid-Life: Psychological and Spiritual Perspectives*. New York: Crossroad, 1982.

Brim, O. G., Jr. "Theories of the Mid-Life Crisis." *The Counseling Psychologist*, 6 (1976), 2–9.

Browning, Don. "Faith and the Dynamics of Knowing." In *The Dialogue Between Theology and Psychology*. Ed. by Peter Homans. Essays in Divinity, III. Chicago: University of Chicago Press, 1968. Pp. 111–34.

Bunyan, John. *The Pilgrim's Progress from this World to That which is to Come*. 2nd ed. Ed. by James B. Wharey and Roger Sharrock. Oxford: Oxford University Press, 1967.

Burrell, David B. "The Church and Individual Life." In *Toward Vatican III: The Work That Needs To Be Done*. Ed. by David Tracy with Hans Küng and Johann B. Metz. New York: Seabury, 1978. Pp. 124–33.

Butler, B. C. "Bernard Lonergan and Conversion." *Worship*, 49 (1975), 329–36.

Caird, G. B. *The Gospel of St. Luke*. The Pelican New Testament Commentaries. Baltimore: Penguin Books, 1963.

Caldwell, Taylor. *Bright Flows the River*. New York: Fawcett Crest, 1978.

Cather, Willa. *The Professor's House*. New York: Vintage Books, 1973.

Colarusso, Calvin A., and Nemiroff, Robert A. *Adult Development: A New Dimension in Psychodynamic Theory and Practice*. New York: Plenum Press, 1981.

Conn, Walter E. "Conversion: A Developmental Perspective." *Cross Currents*, 32 (1982), 323–28.

Connolly, William J. "Contemporary Spiritual Direction: Scope and Principles. An Introductory Essay." *Studies in the Spirituality of Jesuits*, 7 (1975), 95–124.

Conrad, Joseph. *Heart of Darkness and The Secret Sharer*. New York: New American Library, 1910.

Conway, James. *Men in Midlife Crisis*. Elgin, Ill.: Cook, 1978.

Crites, Stephen. "The Narrative Quality of Experience." *Journal of the American Academy of Religion*, 39 (1971), 291–311.

Crossan, John Dominic. *The Dark Interval: Towards a Theology of Story*. Niles, Ill.: Argus, 1975.

Dante Alighieri. *The Divine Comedy of Dante Alighieri*, I: *Inferno*. Trans. by John D. Sinclair. New York: Oxford University Press, 1939.

Davis, Madeleine, and Wallbridge, David. *Boundary and Space: An Introduction to the Work of D. W. Winnicott*. New York: Brunner/Mazel, 1981.

De Sales, Francis. *Introduction to the Devout Life*. Trans. by John K. Ryan. Garden City, N.Y.: Image Books, 1955.

"Direction spirituelle." *Dictionnaire de la Spiritualité Ascetique et Mystique*. III. Paris: Beauchesne, 1957. Cols. 1002–1214.

Dittes, James E. "Beyond William James." In *Beyond the Classics: Essays in the Scientific Study of Religion*. Ed. by C. Y. Glock and Philip Hammond. New York: Harper & Row, 1973. Pp. 291–354.

Doran, Robert. "Psychic Conversion." *The Thomist*, 41 (1977), 200–36.

Dörries, H. "The Place of Confession in Ancient Monasticism." In *Studia Patristica*. Vol. 5. Ed. by F. L. Cross. Berlin: Akademie-Verlag, 1962. Pp. 284–311.

Dulles, Avery. *Models of Revelation*. Garden City, N.Y.: Doubleday, 1983.

Dunne, John. *Time and Myth*. Notre Dame, Ind.: University of Notre Dame Press, 1975.

Dyckman, Katherine Marie, and Carroll, L. Patrick. *Inviting the Mystic, Supporting the Prophet: An Introduction to Spiritual Direction*. New York: Paulist Press, 1981.

Edwards, Tilden H. *Spiritual Friend*. New York: Paulist Press, 1980.

Emerson, Ralph Waldo. *Basic Selections from Emerson*. New York: New American Library, 1954.

English, John. *Choosing Life*. New York: Paulist Press, 1978.

Erikson, Erik H. *Childhood and Society*. 2nd ed. New York: W. W. Norton, 1963.

_____. "Elements of a Psychoanalytic Theory of Psychosocial Development." In *The Course of Life: Psychoanalytic Contributions Toward Understanding Personality Development*. Vol. 1. *Infancy and Early Childhood*. Ed. by Stanley I. Greenspan and George H. Pollock. Washington: US Government Printing Office, 1980. Pp. 11–61.

_____. *Identity and the Life Cycle*. Psychosocial Issues, Vol. 1, no. 1. New York: International Universities Press, 1959.

_____. "Reflections on Dr. Borg's Life Cycle." In *Adulthood*. Ed. by Erik H. Erikson. New York: W. W. Norton, 1978. Pp. 1–31.

_____. *Toys and Reasons: Stages in the Ritualization of Experience*. New York: W. W. Norton, 1977.

Finley, James. *Merton's Place of Nowhere: A Search for God Through Awareness of the True Self*. Notre Dame, Ind.: Ave Maria Press, 1978.

Fischer, Kathleen R. *The Inner Rainbow: The Imagination in Christian Life*. New York: Paulist Press, 1983.

Fiske, Marjorie. "Changing Hierarchies of Commitment in Adulthood." In *Themes of Work and Love in Adulthood*. Ed. by Neil J. Smelser and Erik H. Erikson. Cambridge, Mass.: Harvard University Press, 1980. Pp. 238–64.

Fleming, David L. "Models of Spiritual Direction." *Review for Religious*, 34 (1975), 351–57.

Forsyth, James. "Psychology, Theology, and William James." *Soundings*, 65 (1982), 402–16.

Fowler, James W. "Faith and the Structuring of Meaning." In *Toward Moral and Religious Maturity*. Ed. by James W. Fowler and Antoine Vergote. Morristown, N.J.: Silver Burdett, 1980. Pp. 51–85.

_____. *The Stages of Faith: The Psychology of Human Development and the Quest for Meaning*. San Francisco: Harper & Row, 1981.

Freud, Sigmund. *The Future of an Illusion*. Trans. by W. D. Robson-Scott. Rev. and ed. by James Strachey. Garden City, N.Y.: Anchor Books, 1964.

_____. "Mourning and Melancholia." In *Standard Edition of the Complete Psychological Works of Sigmund Freud*. Ed. by James Strachey. London: Hogarth Press, 1955. Vol. 14.

_____. "Some Reflections on Schoolboy Psychology." In *Standard Edition*. Vol. 13.

Gadamer, Hans-Georg. *Truth and Method*. New York: Continuum, 1975.

141

Geertz, Clifford. "Religion as a Cultural System." In *The Interpretation of Culture*. New York: Basic Books, 1973.

Gilligan, Carol. *In a Different Voice: Psychological Theory and Women's Development*. Cambridge, Mass.: Harvard University Press, 1982.

Gooden, Winston. "Responses from an Adult Development Perspective." In *Faith Development in the Adult Life Cycle*. Ed. by Kenneth Stokes. New York: W. H. Sadlier, 1982.

Gorman, Margaret; Egan, Harvey D.; Going, Catherine M., and Philibert, Paul J. Review symposium on *The Stages of Faith: The Psychology of Human Development and the Quest for Meaning*, by James W. Fowler. *Horizons*, 9 (1982), 104–26.

Gould, Roger L. "Transformations During Early and Middle Adult Years." In *Themes of Work and Love in Adulthood*. Ed. by Neil J. Smelser and Erik H. Erikson. Cambridge, Mass.: Harvard University Press, 1980. Pp. 213–37.

———. *Transformations: Growth and Change in Adult Life*. New York: Simon and Schuster, 1978.

Gratton, Carolyn. *Guidelines for Spiritual Direction*. Studies in Formative Spirituality, 3. Denville, N.J.: Dimension Books, 1980.

Greeley, Andrew. *Religion: A Secular Theory*. New York: Free Press, 1982.

———. *The Religious Imagination*. New York: W. H. Sadlier, 1981.

Greene, Graham. *A Burnt-Out Case*. New York: Viking Press, 1961.

Grolnick, Simon A., and Barkin, Leonard, eds. in collaboration with Werner Muensterberger. *Between Reality and Fantasy: Transitional Objects and Phenomena*. New York: Jason Aronson, 1978.

Groome, Thomas H. *Christian Religious Education: Sharing Our Story and Vision*. San Francisco: Harper & Row, 1980.

Guillet, Jacques et al. *Discernment of Spirits*. Trans. by Innocentia Richards. Collegeville, Minn.: Liturgical Press, 1970.

Guntrip, Harry. *Psychoanalytic Theory, Therapy, and the Self: A Basic Guide to the Human Personality in Freud, Erikson, Klein, Sullivan, Fairbairn, Hartmann, Jacobson, and Winnicott*. New York: Basic Books, 1973.

———. "Religion in Relation to Personal Integration." *British Journal of Medical Psychology*, 42 (1969), 323–33.

Gustafson, James M. "Moral Discernment in the Christian Life." In *Norm and Context in Christian Ethics*. Ed. by Gene Outka and Paul Ramsey. New York: Scribners, 1968. Pp. 17–36.

Hannah, Barbara. *Encounters with the Soul: Active Imagination as Developed by C. G. Jung*. Santa Monica, Cal.: Sigo Press, 1981.

Harned, David Baily. *Images for Self-Recognition: The Christian as Player, Sufferer, and Vandal*. New York: Seabury, 1977.

Hart, Ray L. *The Unfinished Man and the Imagination*. New York: Herder and Herder, 1968.

Hauerwas, Stanley. *Truthfulness and Tragedy*. Notre Dame, Ind.: University of Notre Dame Press, 1977.

Haughey, John C. *The Conspiracy of God: The Holy Spirit in Men*. Garden City, N.Y.: Doubleday, 1973.

Herrigel, Eugen. *Zen in the Art of Archery.* Trans. by R. F. C. Hull. New York: Vintage Books, 1971.

Hiltner, Seward. "Toward Autonomous Pastoral Diagnosis." *Bulletin of the Menninger Clinic,* 40 (1976), 573–92.

Hilton, Walter. *The Scale of Perfection.* Abridged and presented by Illtyd Tretho- wan. St. Meinrad, Ind.: Abbey Press, 1975.

Holmes, Urban T., III. *Ministry and Imagination.* New York: Seabury, 1976.

Homans, Peter. "Psychology and Hermeneutics: An Exploration of Basic Issues and Resources." *Journal of Religion,* 55 (1975), 327–47.

Horowitz, Mardi Jon. *Image Formation and Psychotherapy.* New York: Jason Aronson, 1983.

Horton, Paul C. *Solace: The Missing Dimension in Psychiatry.* Chicago: Univer- sity of Chicago Press, 1981.

Ignatius Loyola. *The Spiritual Exercises of St. Ignatius.* Trans. by Anthony Mottola. Garden City, N.Y.: Doubleday, 1964.

Isabell, Damien. *The Spiritual Director: A Practical Guide.* Chicago: Franciscan Herald Press, 1976.

Jacobi, Jolande. *Complex-Archetype-Symbol in the Psychology of C. G. Jung.* Trans. by Ralph Manheim. Bollingen Series, 57. New York: Pantheon Books, 1959.

James, William. *The Varieties of Religious Experience: A Study in Human Nature.* New York: Collier Books, 1961.

Jaques, Elliott. "Death and the Mid-Life Crisis." In *The Interpretation of Death.* Ed. by Hendrik M. Ruitenbeek. New York: Jason Aronson, 1973. Pp. 140– 65.

———. "The Midlife Crisis." In *The Course of Life: Psychoanalytic Contributions Toward Understanding Personality Development.* Vol. 3. *Adulthood and the Aging Process.* Ed. by Stanley I. Greenspan and George H. Pollock. Washington: US Government Printing Office, 1980. Pp. 1–23.

John of the Cross. *The Collected Works of St. John of the Cross.* Trans. by Kieran Kavanaugh and Otilio Rodriguez. Washington: ICS Publications, 1973.

Johnston, William. *The Inner Eye of Love: Mysticism and Religion.* San Francisco: Harper & Row, 1978.

Jones, Alan. *Exploring Spiritual Direction: An Essay on Christian Friendship.* New York: Seabury, 1982.

Jung, Carl G. *Aion: Researches into the Phenomenology of the Self.* 2nd ed. Trans. by R. F. C. Hull. Bollingen Series, 20. Princeton, N.J.: Princeton Univer- sity Press, 1959.

———. *Analytical Psychology: Its Theory and Practice.* New York: Random House, 1970.

———. *Modern Man in Search of a Soul.* Trans. by W. S. Dell and Cary F. Baynes. New York: Harcourt, Brace & World, 1933.

———. *Psychology and Religion: West and East.* Trans. by R. F. C. Hull. Bollingen Series, 11. New York: Pantheon Books, 1958.

———. *The Undiscovered Self.* Trans. by R. F. C. Hull. New York: New American Library, 1957.

Kelsey, Morton T. *Christo-Psychology*. New York: Crossroad, 1982.

——. *Companions on the Inner Way: The Art of Spiritual Guidance*. New York: Crossroad, 1983.

Kernberg, Otto. *Internal World and External Reality: Object Relations Theory Applied*. New York: Jason Aronson, 1980.

King, Eugene W. "A Pastoral Theological Reflection on Storytelling." *Chicago Studies*, 21 (1982), 7–21.

Klein, Melanie. *Envy and Gratitude and Other Works: 1946–1963*. New York: Dell, 1977.

Kort, Wesley A. *Narrative Elements and Religious Meaning*. Philadelphia: Fortress Press, 1975.

Küng, Hans. *Freud and the Problem of God*. Trans. by Edward Quinn. New Haven: Yale University Press, 1979.

Ladner, Gerhart B. *The Idea of Reform: Its Impact on Christian Thought and Action in the Age of the Fathers*. Cambridge, Mass.: Harvard University Press, 1959.

Lane, Dermot A. *The Experience of God: An Invitation to Do Theology*. New York: Paulist Press, 1981.

Laplace, Jean. *Preparing for Spiritual Direction*. Trans. by John C. Guinness. Chicago: Franciscan Herald Press, 1975.

Leech, Kenneth. *Soul Friend: A Study of Spirituality*. London: Sheldon Press, 1977.

Levinson, Daniel J. "Toward a Conception of the Adult Life Course." In *Themes of Work and Love in Adulthood*. Ed. by Neil J. Smelser and Erik H. Erikson. Cambridge, Mass.: Harvard University Press, 1980. Pp. 265–90.

Levinson, Daniel J., et al. *The Seasons of a Man's Life*. New York: Alfred A. Knopf, 1978.

Lienhard, Joseph T. "On 'Discernment of Spirits' in the Early Church." *Theological Studies*, 41 (1980), 505–29.

Loder, James E. *The Transforming Moment: Understanding Convictional Experiences*. San Francisco: Harper & Row, 1981.

Loder, James E., and Fowler, James W. "Conversations on Fowler's *Stages of Faith* and Loder's *The Transforming Moment*." *Religious Education*, 77 (1982), 133–48.

Lonergan, Bernard. *Method in Theology*. New York: Herder and Herder, 1972.

——. "Theology in Its New Context." In *A Second Collection*. Ed. by William F. J. Ryan and Bernard J. Tyrrell. London: Darton, Longman & Todd, 1974. Pp. 55–67.

Louf, André. *Teach Us to Pray*. Trans. by Hubert Hoskins. New York: Paulist Press, 1975.

Lowe, Walter. "Psychoanalysis as an Archeology of the History of Suffering." In *The Challenge of Psychology to Faith*. Concilium, 156. Ed. by Steven Kepnes and David Tracy. New York: Seabury, 1982. Pp. 3–9.

Lynch, William. *Images of Faith: An Exploration of the Ironic Imagination*. Notre Dame, Ind.: University of Notre Dame Press, 1973.

———. *Images of Hope: Imagination as Healer of the Hopeless*. Notre Dame, Ind.: University of Notre Dame Press, 1974.

McBride, Alfred. "Reaction to Fowler: Fears About Procedure." In *Values and Moral Development*. Ed. by Thomas C. Hennessy. New York: Paulist Press, 1976. Pp. 211–18.

McCready, William G. "Religion and the Life Cycle." In *Toward Vatican III: The Work That Needs to Be Done*. Ed. by David Tracy with Hans Küng and Johann B. Metz. New York: Seabury, 1978. Pp. 272–87.

McFague, Sallie. "Conversion: Life on the Edge of the Raft." *Interpretation*, 32 (1978), 255–68.

McGill, Michael E. *The 40- to 60-Year Old Male: A Guide for Men—and the Women in Their Lives—to See Them Through the Crises of the Male Middle Years*. New York: Simon and Schuster, 1980.

McNeill, John T. *A History of the Cure of Souls*. New York: Harper & Row, 1951.

Marmor, Judd. "The Crisis of Middle Age." In *Psychiatry in Transition*. New York: Brunner/Mazel, 1974. Pp. 71–76.

Martin, Gerhard Marcel. *Fest: The Transformation of Everyday*. Trans. by M. Douglas Meeks. Philadelphia: Fortress Press, 1976.

May, Gerald G. *Care of Mind/Care of Spirit: Psychiatric Dimensions of Spiritual Direction*. San Francisco: Harper & Row, 1982.

———. *Will and Spirit: A Contemplative Psychology*. San Francisco: Harper & Row, 1982.

May, Rollo. *The Courage to Create*. New York: Bantam, 1976.

———. *Love and Will*. New York: Dell, 1969.

Mayer, Nancy. *The Male Mid-Life Crisis*. New York: Viking Press, 1978.

Meissner, W. W. "Notes on the Psychology of Faith." *Journal of Religion and Health*, 8 (1969), 47–75.

———. "Psychoanalytic Aspects of Religious Experience." *Annual of Psychoanalysis*, 6 (1978), 103–41.

———. "The Psychology of Religious Experience." *Communio*, 4 (1977), 36–59.

Menninger, Karl, with Martin Mayman and Paul Pruyser. *The Vital Balance: The Life Process in Mental Health and Illness*. New York: Penguin Books, 1963.

Merton, Thomas. *Contemplative Prayer*. Garden City, N.Y.: Image Books, 1971.

———. "Final Integration: Toward a Monastic Therapy." In *Contemplation in a World of Action*. Garden City, N.Y.: Image Books, 1973. Pp. 219–31.

———. "Is the Contemplative Life Finished?" In *Contemplation in a World of Action*. Pp. 343–96.

———. *New Seeds of Contemplation*. New York: New Directions, 1961.

———. *Spiritual Direction and Meditation*. Collegeville, Minn.: Liturgical Press, 1960.

———. "The Spiritual Father in the Desert Tradition." In *Contemplation in a World of Action*. Pp. 282–305.

Miller, Alice. *Prisoners of Childhood*. Trans. by Ruth Ward. New York: Basic Books, 1981.

Mogul, Kathleen M. "Women in Midlife: Decisions, Rewards, and Conflicts Related to Work and Careers." *American Journal of Psychiatry*, 136 (1979), 1139–43.

Moran, Gabriel. "Responses from the Religious Education Perspective." In *Faith Development in the Adult Life Cycle*. Ed. by Kenneth Stokes. New York: W. H. Sadlier, 1982. Pp. 149–77.

Murphy, Sheila. "Women's Midlife Mourning: The Wake of Youth." *Human Development*, 2 (1981), 21–26.

Neugarten, Bernice L. "Time, Age, and the Life Cycle." *American Journal of Psychiatry*, 136 (1979), 887–94.

Neuman, Matthias. "Self-Identity, Symbol, and Imagination: Some Implications of Their Interaction for Christian Sacramental Theology." In *Symbolisme et Théologie*. Studia Anselmiana, 64. Rome: Editrice Anselmiana, 1975. Pp. 91–123.

Nicene and Post-Nicene Fathers. 2nd series. Reprint. Grand Rapids: Eerdmans, 1973.

Niebuhr, H. Richard. *The Responsible Self: An Essay in Christian Moral Philosophy*. New York: Harper & Row, 1963.

Norman, William H., and Scaramella, Thomas J., eds. *Mid-Life: Developmental and Clinical Issues*. New York: Brunner/Mazel, 1980.

Notman, Malkah. "Midlife Concerns of Women: Implications of the Menopause." *American Journal of Psychiatry*, 136 (1979), 1270–74.

Nouwen, Henri J. M. "Hospitality." *Monastic Studies*, 10 (1974), 1–28.

_____. *The Living Reminder: Service and Prayer in Memory of Jesus Christ*. New York: Seabury, 1977.

O'Collins, Gerald. *The Second Journey*. New York: Paulist Press, 1978.

Otto, Rudolf. *The Idea of the Holy: An Inquiry into the Non-Rational Factor in the Idea of the Divine and Its Relation to the Rational*. Trans. by John W. Harvey. Oxford: Oxford University Press, 1950.

Pasquier, Jacques. "Experience and Conversion." *The Way*, 17 (1977), 114–22.

Peck, M. Scott. *The Road Less Traveled: A New Psychology of Love, Traditional Values and Spiritual Growth*. New York: Simon and Schuster, 1978.

Peck, Robert C. "Psychological Developments in the Second Half of Life." In *Middle Age and Aging*. Ed. by Bernice L. Neugarten. Chicago: University of Chicago Press, 1968. Pp. 88–92.

Proust, Marcel. *Remembrance of Things Past*. Vol. 2. Trans. by C. K. S. Moncrieff. London: Chatto and Windus, 1968.

Pruyser, Paul W. *Between Belief and Unbelief*. New York: Harper & Row, 1974.

_____. "An Essay on Creativity." *Bulletin of the Menninger Clinic*, 43 (1979), 294–353.

_____. "Forms and Functions of the Imagination in Religion." Photocopy.

_____. *The Minister as Diagnostician: Personal Problems in Pastoral Perspective*. Philadelphia: Westminster Press, 1976.

_____. "Narcissism in Contemporary Religion." *Journal of Pastoral Care*, 32 (1978), 219–31.

146

Puzon, Bridget. "The *Bildungsroman* of Middle Life." *Harvard Library Bulletin,* 26 (1978), 5–27.

———. "The Hidden Meaning in *Humphrey Clinker.*" *Harvard Library Bulletin,* 24 (1976), 40–54.

Raabe, Augusta. "Discernment of Spirits in the Prologue to the *Rule of Benedict.*" *American Benedictine Review,* 23 (1972), 397–423.

Rahner, Hugo. *Ignatius the Theologian.* Trans. by Michael Barry. New York: Herder and Herder, 1968.

Rahner, Karl. "Comments by Karl Rahner on Questions Raised by Avery Dulles." In *Ignatius of Loyola: His Personality and Spiritual Heritage, 1556–1956.* Ed. by Friedrich Wulf. St. Louis: Institute of Jesuit Sources, 1977. Pp. 290–93.

———. " 'He Descended into Hell.' " In *Theological Investigations.* Vol. 7: *Further Theology of the Spiritual Life I.* Trans. by David Bourke. New York: Herder and Herder, 1971. Pp. 145–50.

———. "Experience of the Holy Spirit." In *Theological Investigations.* Vol. 18: *God and Revelation.* Trans. by Edward Quinn. New York: Crossroad, 1983. Pp. 189–210.

———. "Ideas for a Theology of Childhood." In *Theological Investigations.* Vol. 8: *Further Theology of the Spiritual Life 2.* Trans. by David Bourke. New York: Herder and Herder, 1971. Pp. 33–50.

———. "The Ignatian Process for Discovering the Will of God in an Existential Situation: Some Theological Problems in the Rules for Election and Discernment of Spirits in St. Ignatius' *Spiritual Exercises.*" In *Ignatius of Loyola: His Personality and Spiritual Heritage, 1556–1956.* Pp. 280–89.

Ricoeur, Paul. *Freud and Philosophy: An Essay on Interpretation.* Trans. by Denis Savage. New Haven: Yale University Press, 1970.

———. *Hermeneutics and the Human Sciences: Essays on Language, Action and Interpretation.* Ed. and trans. by John B. Thompson. Cambridge: Cambridge University Press, 1981.

———. *Interpretation Theory: Discourse and the Surplus of Meaning.* Fort Worth: Tex.: Texas Christian University Press, 1976.

———. "Listening to the Parables of Jesus." In *The Philosophy of Paul Ricoeur: An Anthology of His Work.* Ed. by Charles E. Regan and David Stewart. Boston: Beacon Press, 1978. Pp. 239–45.

———. *The Symbolism of Evil.* Trans. by Emerson Buchanan. New York: Harper & Row, 1967.

Rizzuto, Ana-Maria. *The Birth of the Living God: A Psychoanalytic Study.* Chicago: University of Chicago Press, 1979.

Robb, Paul V. "Conversion as a Human Experience." *Studies in the Spirituality of Jesuits,* 14 (1982), no. 3.

Rogers, Kenn. "The Mid-Career Crisis." *Saturday Review of Society,* 1 (1973), 37–38.

Rubin, Lillian. *Women of a Certain Age: The Midlife Search for Self.* New York: Harper & Row, 1979.

Sammon, Sean D. "Life After Youth: The Midlife Transition and Its Aftermath." *Human Development*, 3 (1982), 15–25.

The Sayings of the Desert Fathers: The Alphabetical Collection. Trans. by Benedicta Ward. London: A. R. Mowbray, 1975.

Schafer, Roy. *A New Language for Psychoanalysis*. New Haven: Yale University Press, 1976.

Schneiders, Sandra M. "The Contemporary Ministry of Direction." *Chicago Studies*, 15 (1976), 119–135.

———. *Spiritual Direction: Reflections on a Contemporary Ministry*. Chicago: National Sisters Vocation Conference, 1977.

———. "Spiritual Discernment in *The Dialogue* of Saint Catherine of Siena." *Horizons*, 9 (1982), 47–59.

Searle, Mark. "The Journey of Conversion." *Worship*, 54 (1980), 35–55.

Segal, Hanna. *Introduction to the Work of Melanie Klein*. 2nd ed. New York: Basic Books, 1974.

Settlage, Calvin F. "Cultural Values and the Superego in Late Adolescence." *The Psychoanalytic Study of the Child*, 27 (1972), 74–92.

Shea, John. *Stories of God: An Unauthorized Biography*. Chicago: Thomas More Press, 1978.

Sheehy, Gail. *Passages: Predictable Crises of Adult Life*. New York: Bantam Books, 1976.

Sobel, Emilie. "Rhythm, Sound and Imagery in the Poetry of Gerard Manley Hopkins." In *Between Reality and Fantasy: Transitional Objects and Phenomena*. Ed. by Simon A. Grolnick and Leonard Barkin in collaboration with Werner Muensterberger. New York: Jason Aronson, 1978. Pp. 427–45.

Sobrino, Jon. "Following Jesus as Discernment." *Concilium*, 119 (1978), 14–24.

Spencer, Anita. *Seasons: Women's Search for Self Through Life's Stages*. New York: Paulist Press, 1982.

Spohn, William C. "The Reasoning Heart: An American Approach to Christian Discernment." *Theological Studies*, 44 (1983), 30–52.

Steele, Robert S. *Freud and Jung: Conflicts of Interpretation*. London: Routledge & Kegan Paul, 1982.

Steere, Douglas. "On Listening to Another." In *The Doubleday Devotional Classics*. Vol. 3. Ed. by E. Glenn Hinson. Garden City, N.Y.: Doubleday, 1978.

Stein, Edith. *The Science of the Cross*. Trans. by Hilda Graef. Chicago: H. Regnery, 1960.

Stinnette, Charles R., Jr. "Reflection and Transformation: Knowing and Change in Psychotherapy and in Religious Faith." In *The Dialogue Between Theology and Psychology*. Essays in Divinity, III. Ed. by Peter Homans. Chicago: University of Chicago Press, 1968. Pp. 83–110.

Stokes, Kenneth, ed. *Faith Development in the Adult Life Cycle*. New York: W. H. Sadlier, 1982.

Stroup, George W. *The Promise of Narrative Theology: Recovering the Gospel in the Church*. Atlanta: John Knox Press, 1981.

Studzinski, Raymond. "The Minister of Reconciliation: Some Historical Models." In *Background and Directions. The Rite of Penance: Commentaries.* Vol. 3. Ed. by Nathan Mitchell. Washington: Liturgical Conference, 1978. Pp. 50–61.

Tracy, David. *The Analogical Imagination: Christian Theology and the Culture of Pluralism.* New York: Crossroad, 1981.

Turner, Victor. "Passages, Margins, and Poverty: Religious Symbols of Communitas." In *Dramas, Fields, and Metaphors: Symbolic Action in Human Society.* Ithaca: Cornell University Press, 1974. Pp. 231–71.

———. *The Ritual Process: Structure and Anti-Structure.* Chicago: Aldine, 1969.

Ulanov, Ann. Review of *The Birth of the Living God: A Psychoanalytic Study,* by Ana-Maria Rizzuto. *Union Seminary Quarterly Review,* 36 (1981), 173–76.

Ulanov, Ann, and Ulanov, Barry. *Primary Speech: A Psychology of Prayer.* Atlanta: John Knox Press, 1982.

Vaillant, George E. *Adaptation to Life.* Boston: Little, Brown and Co., 1977.

———. "Adaptation to Life." A presentation at "In Celebration of Life Transitions," a conference sponsored by the Continuing Education Department of the University of Kansas and The Center for Applied Behavioral Sciences of The Menninger Foundation, 1980. Audiotape.

Vaillant, George E., and McArthur, Charles A. "Natural History of Male Psychologic Health. I. The Adult Life Cycle from 18–50." *Seminars in Psychiatry,* 4 (1972), 415–27.

Vanderwall, Francis W. *Spiritual Direction: An Invitation to Abundant Life.* New York: Paulist Press, 1981.

Van Gennep, Arnold. *The Rites of Passage.* Chicago: University of Chicago Press, 1960.

Van Kaam, Adrian. *The Dynamics of Spiritual Self Direction.* Denville, N.J.: Dimension Books, 1976.

———. *In Search of Spiritual Identity.* Denville, N.J.: Dimension Books, 1975.

Wathen, Ambrose. "The Exigencies of Benedict's Little Rule for Beginners— RB 72." *American Benedictine Review,* 29 (1978), 41–66.

Wheelis, Allen. *The Scheme of Things.* New York: Harcourt Brace Jovanovich, 1980.

Whitehead, Alfred North. *Adventures of Ideas.* New York: Macmillan, 1933.

———. *Process and Reality: An Essay in Cosmology.* New York: Macmillan, 1929.

Whitehead, Evelyn Eaton, and Whitehead, James D. *Christian Life Patterns: The Psychological Challenges and Religious Invitations of Adult Life.* Garden City, N.Y.: Doubleday, 1979.

Wilkes, J. R. "Remembering." *Theology,* 84 (1981), 87–95.

Winnicott, D. W. "Creativity and Its Origins." In *Playing and Reality.* London: Tavistock Publications, 1971. Pp. 65–85.

———. "Ego Distortion in Terms of True and False Self." In *The Maturational Processes and the Facilitating Environment.* New York: International Universities Press, 1965. Pp. 140–52.

———. "Playing: Creative Activity and the Search for the Self." In *Playing and Reality.* Pp. 53–64.

_____. "Transitional Objects and Transitional Phenomena." In *Playing and Reality*. Pp. 1–25.

The Wisdom of the Desert: Sayings from the Desert Fathers of the Fourth Century. Trans. by Thomas Merton. New York: New Directions, 1960.

Wright, John H. *A Theology of Christian Prayer.* New York: Pueblo, 1979.

Wuthnow, Robert. "A Sociological Perspective on Faith Development." In *Faith Development in the Adult Life Cycle.* Ed. by Kenneth Stokes. New York: W. H. Sadlier, 1982. Pp. 209–43.

Zullo, James R. "The Crisis of Limits: Midlife Beginnings." *Human Development*, 3 (1982), 6–14.

Index

Acceptance, 39, 41
Adaptation to Life (George Valliant), 30
Adaptive mechanisms, 30
Adolescence, 41
Adult development, 28–34
Adulthood, ethical rule of, 39
Aging process, 35
Ambivalence, 39, 45
Ambivalent feeling, 37
Anxiety, 35, 38
Apathetic surrender, 38
Apprenticeship, 48
The Ascent of Mount Carmel (St. John of the Cross), 17

Bergman, Ingmar, 46
Bodily appearance, 38
Bodily changes, 41
Bright Flows the River (Taylor Caldwell), 57
Browning, Don, 133
A Burnt-Out Case (Graham Greene), 1, 134
Burrell, David, 51

Care, 39, 45, 128
"Career consolidation," 30
Cassian, John, 75–76
Cather, Willa, 103
Christian life, virtues of, 77
Church, 51–52
  rituals and symbols of, 101
Church, Richard, 33

Commitment, 23
Conflict, 20
Conn, Walter E., 58
Conversion, 56–71; *see also* Midlife: conversion
  life-long process, 13
  types of, 14
  turmoil and turbulance of, 14
  understanding of, 13
Counseling, 6
Creativity, 34, 129, 130–131
Crisis, 33–34, 70–71
Crites, Stephen, 110
Cross, 23

Dante Alighieri, 15, 23
Dark night, 15–16, 70
"Deadline decade," 41
Death
  acceptance of, 22, 44
  and rebirth, 21
  fear of, 39
  inevitability of, 2
  reality of, 23
"Death and the Mid-Life Crisis" (Elliott Jaques), 34
Decision-making, 8, 77
Decompensation, 38
Defense mechanisms, 30–31
Denial, 38
Dependence, 108
Depression, 35, 38, 96
Depressive anxiety, 37, 39
"Depressive position," 36, 38

Despair, 46
Destructiveness, 35, 36, 38
Detachment, 39
Developmental psychology, 12, 52
Developmental tasks, 28–29
Discernment, 8, 70–78
The Divine Comedy (Dante Alighieri), 15
Dunne, John, 112

Ego, 30–31
Emerson, Ralph Waldo, 87
Emotional exhaustion, 37
Envy, 38, 42
Erikson, Erik H., 29–30, 38–39, 45–47,
  66, 71, 93, 130, 132

Failure, sense of, 39
Faith
  as commitment, 23
  development, stages, of, 65–69
  journey in, 21
  purified, 16
Faith-work, 69–70
Fantasy, 35, 87
Fiske, Marjorie, 44
Fowler, James, 64–68, 98
Francis de Sales, 124
Freud, Sigmund, 7, 106–7, 125
Friendship, 124

Generational cycle, 46
Generativity, 45
Gilligan, Carol, 32, 45
God
  and deeper self, 104
  as Father, 106–7
  beyond images, 103, 104, 108–9
  childish notions of, 22–23
  concept of, 105–6
  core-image of, 107
  distance or absence of, 103, 104, 108–9
  images of, 9, 40, 84–85, 99, 105–8
  relationship to, 9, 92, 96, 105, 107, 134
Gooden, Winston, 69–70
Gould, Roger, 47–48, 94
Grace, 51, 132, 136
Grant Study, 30, 33

Gratitude, 38
Greeley, Andrew, 105
Gregory of Nyssa, 84
Grief, 38
Guilt, 38
Guntrip, Harry, 109, 125, 126

Hate, 36, 38–39
Hauerwas, Stanley, 110
Healthy minded, 59
Heart
  and contemplation, 85
  inner workings of, 83
Heart of Darkness (Joseph Conrad), 63
Helping professions, 123
Hermeneutic circle, 98
Hermeneutical theory, 78; *see also*
  Interpretation theory
Herrigel, Eugen, 101
Hidden agendas, 125
Hilton, Walter, 84
Holiness, 122
Holy Spirit, 52, 134, 135; *see also* Spirit
Homans, Peter, 98
Hope, 38
Hopkins, Gerard Manley, 85, 89
Humanity
  and Jesus Christ, 99
  transcendent goal of, 100

The Idea of the Holy (Rudolf Otto), 88
Ideal self, 93
Ideals
  and symbols, 92
  fidelity to, 43
Identification, 40
Identity
  and personal history, 96–98
  existential, 93
  formation, 93, 97
  new interpretations of, 98
  spiritual, 93
Ignatius Loyola, 10, 74–75
Illusion, 87
  and transcendent, 87
  capacity for, 90
  formation, 89
  processing of, 91

Images, 93–110
    and illusions, 89
    and symbols, 65
    inadequate or evil, 99
    master, 102–3
    negative and positive, 93–94
    of God, 108, 109–10
    of self, 93–94, 96, 103, 110
    of self and God, 92
Imagination, 87–88
    and contemplative life, 85–86
    and reason, 97
    as conscious and unconscious process,
        62
    creative, 87
    ironic, 67
    working of, 85
Immortality, fantasy of, 35
Imperfection, recognition of, 69
In a Different Voice (Carol Gilligan), 32
Independence, relative, 108
Individuation
    and midlife, 42
    movement toward, 48–49
    process of, 29
Insight, 62
Integration, 20, 38
Integrity
    achievement of, 46
    sense of, 29
Intentional interpretation, 114
Internalization, 40
Interpretation theory, 98
Intuition, 62

James, William, 59, 60–61
Jaques, Elliott, 36, 39
Jesus Christ
    and conversion, 71, 72
    and discernment, 72
    and the Father, 71
    as a key image, 99–100
John of the Cross, 14–17, 70, 122
Johnston, William, 20–21, 22
Journey metaphor, 17–18
"The Journey of Conversion" (Mark
    Searle), 17
Judgment
    evaluative, 78

    hermeneutical, 78
    practical, 78
Jung, Carl, 14, 21, 28, 57, 85, 100

Kernberg, Otto, 45
King, Edward, 113
Kingdom of God, 65, 73, 128
Klein, Melanie, 36, 47
Knowing
    convictional, 64
    transformational, 62–63
Küng, Hans, 106

Leech, Kenneth, 7
Letting go, 96
Levinson, Daniel J., 31–33, 35, 43, 47,
    48–49, 92
Life
    Christian vision of, 132
    "noon" of, 28
    playful attitude toward, 102
Life cycle, 46, 47
The Life of Antony (St. Athanasius), 76
Life story, 115
Life structure, 31–32
Liminality, 100
Limits, 36, 41
Listening, 115
The Living Reminder (Henri Nouwen),
    136
Loder, James E., 61, 62–64
Loneliness, 47, 64
Lonergan, Bernard, 13
Loss, 37, 44, 96
Love, 39, 122

Marmor, Judd, 35, 38
Master-image, 102–3; *see also* Images
May, Gerald, 106
May, Rollo, 128
Meissner, William W., 52, 87, 105, 108
Memories, 37, 97, 112, 135
Menopause, 35
Mentor, 47, 48–49
Merton, Thomas, 7, 14, 85, 104, 109
Midlife
    and demonic, 99

and divided self, 59–61
and one's childhood, 97, 129
assessment of talents, 41
balancing polarities, 42
boredom and frustration, 91
conversion, 14–15, 56–71, 114
faith, 64–70
interiority, 85
self-surrender, 101–2
turbulence, 32, 35
Midlife crisis, 3, 33, 43, 70
Midlife transition, 3, 32–33, 40, 42, 50, 70
Modern Man in Search of a Soul (Carl Jung), 11
Moral choices, 77
Moratoria, 44
Mourning, 35, 37, 45, 96
Mourning and Melancholia (Sigmund Freud), 45

Narcissism, 103, 108
Neugarten, Bernice, 33, 111
New Seeds of Contemplation (Thomas Merton), 60
Niebuhr, H. Richard, 103
"Normal Narcissism in Middle Age" (Otto Kernberg), 45
Nouwen, Henri, 128, 136

Object relations theory, 36, 107
O'Collins, Gerald, 18–19
Old age, concern about, 41
"On the Sense of Loneliness" (Melanie Klein), 47
Open stories, 114–15
Origen, 84
Otto, Rudolf, 88
Over-beliefs, 61
Overcompensation, 38

Parables, 57, 86, 88, 108
Parents
    and children, 45
    death of, 44–45, 106
    love of, 39
    relationships to, 35, 45

Passages (Gail Sheehy), 10
Peck, M. Scott, 77
Personal history, 98
Personal myths, 42
Physical deterioration, 35
Pilgrim's Progress (Paul Bunyan), 3
Play
    adult form, 129
    and childhood, 129
    and fairness, 102
    and religious rituals, 130
    creative, 129
Polarities, balancing of, 32
Prayer
    and asceticism, 76
    and images, 104
    and memories, 97
    distractions in, 95
    feeling states in, 105
    mystical, 20
The Professor's House (Willa Cather), 103
Proust, Marcel, 36
Providence, 132
Pruyser, Paul, 51, 89, 90, 130
Purification, process of, 10
Purity of heart, 134

Rage, 38
Rahner, Karl, 23, 75, 129, 135
Rationality, 60
Reaction patterns to loss, 37–38
Reality, 67, 89, 91
    psychoanalytic vision of, 131
"Reflections on Dr. Borg's Life Cycle" (Erik Erikson), 46
Remembrance of Things Past (Marcel Proust), 36
Reparation, 37
Repentance, 77, 132
Responsibility, 39
Ricoeur, Paul, 67, 88, 98
Rizzuto, Ana-Maria, 107, 109
The Road Less Traveled (M. Scott Peck), 77
Rule of Benedict, 72, 74

Sacred stories, 112–15
Salvation, 5, 86
Schafer, Roy, 131

The Scheme of Things (Allen Wheelis), 62
Schleiermacher, Friedrich, 88
Schneiders, Sandra, 78
Sculpted creativity, 34
The Seasons of a Man's Life (Daniel Levinson), 31
"Second adolescence," 35
"Second Naïveté," 67
Self
  attitude toward, 102
  childhood senses of, 94
  deeper levels of, 85, 103
  divided, 59–61
  false, 60, 75, 95
  ideal images of, 95
  images of, 78, 93–94, 95, 103, 104–105
  mystery of, 104
  narcissistic distortions of, 95
  social, 103
  transcendence of, 115
  true, 60, 104
  wounded, 86
Self-acceptance, 42
Self-deception, 78
Self-definition, 48
Self-denial, 128
Self-esteem, 124
Self-image
  and God-images, 104–5
  and identity, 96
  positive and negative, 93
  selective, 114
Self-surrender, 102
Self-transcendence, 62
Sexual feelings, 105, 127
Shadow, 69, 94
Shea, John, 113–14
Sick-minded, 59
Sinful tendencies, 95
Sobrino, Jon, 71–72
Soul Friend (Kenneth Leech), 7
Spirit; *see also* Holy Spirit
  experiences of, 135–36
Spirits, good and evil, 76
Spiritual awakening, 10
Spritual direction, 5–7, 123–36
  and creativity, 129
  and decision-making, 8
  and perspectives on midlife, 50
  as play, 129–31

central issues in, 8
in relation to psychotherapy and
  counseling, 6–8
Spiritual director
  and developmental psychology, 52
  as facilitator, 4
  preparation of, 4
  qualities of, 5–6, 124
  vision of, 131
Spiritual Exercises (Ignatius Loyola) 10, 74
Spiritual theology, 11, 51
Spohn, William, 112
Stage theory
  and hermeneutical styles, 98
  developmental (Erikson), 29–30
  of faith (Fowler), 65–69, 70
The Stages of Faith (James Fowler), 64
Steele, Robert, 111
Steere, Douglas, 115
Stein, Edith, 15
Story, 110–15
Storytelling, 110–11, 115
Stress, 35
Sublimation, 37
Suffering
  and sin, 114
  legitimate, 126
  painful roots of, 111–12
Symbols
  and ideals, 92
  and images, 65
  as context for growth, 99
  Christian tradition and, 77
  conceptual meaning of, 67

Teresa of Avila, 10
Therapy, 6–8, 123
Time, perspectives on, 40
Tranquility, 134
Transference, 125
Transformation, 47–49
  process of, in faith work, 70
Transformations (Roger Gould), 47
The Transforming Moment (James Loder), 61
Transition from doing to suffering, 14
Trust
  mature, 108
  versus mistruct, 66

Truth
about self, 8, 97
quest for, 95

Unconscious
and conscious, 62
and holy, 61
conflicts, 35
memories, 37
The Undiscovered Self (Carl Jung), 69
Unrealistic expectations in direction, 125

Vaillant, George, 29–31, 33, 40, 47, 48,
97
The Varieties of Religious Experience
(William James), 59
Vision, ironic and tragic, 132
Van Gennep, Arnold, 100
Vocation, 132

The Voyage Home (Richard Church), 33

Wheelis, Allen, 62
Wholeness, 39, 46, 64
"Wild Strawberries" (Ingmar Bergman),
46
Willfulness and willingness, 102
Winnicott, D. W., 49, 89–90, 130–31
Wisdom, 39, 46
Women's development, 32–33, 45
Working through, 38
World
autistic, 97
external, 89
illusionistic, 90–92
inner, 90

Zen, and Zen masters, 101